PRAISE FOR
The Paradoxical Return of the Feminine

"For decades Gagan's clarion voice has called us beyond psychological tenets and repairs to navigate the mystery of how to come alive to our deepest selves. In *Paradoxical Return of the Feminine*, she weaves potent metaphor and her own true, intimate story to draw us into a fuller understanding of ways to call our souls back home, along with some practical tools for doing so. Encouraging and wise, she offers possibilities to both men and women to find that genderless depth of the feminine in all of life that can return compassion and peace in fuller measure to our world."
Cecile Carson, MD, founding board member of the
Society for Shamanic Practitioners

"Dr. Jeannette Gagan's insightful words are a balm for today's growing, heated conflicts among races and religions. We follow her through her personal struggles and healing from youthful spiritual and emotional wounds to her eventual growth in accepting her own feminine beauty and power. She leads us step by step in recognizing that the Return of the Feminine is a matter of both women and men finding the balance of their masculine and within—and then actualizing it without—in the realization of our interconnectedness with all life."
Vijali Hamilton, MFA, founding director the World Wheel Project,
Global Peace through the Arts, author, and filmmaker

"Dr. Jeannette Gagan is one of the inspirational women who are actively engaging in lifting the level of awareness and peace on our planet. Her most recent book delivers many pragmatic, attainable ways to achieve this. I applaud her efforts!"
Dr. Paula Fellingham, Global Prosperity and Peace Mentor

"Having always known that I possessed an inner Goddess, only recently have I allowed myself to celebrate her. Jeannette has gracefully captured the journey that has been and is feminism. She writes with an easy, complicated, yet organized manner. As part of this amazing tribe of women, I urge you to devour, underline, highlight, and post to your mirror quotations from Jeannette that inspire you. Embrace the wonderful uniqueness of EVERY female you encounter—but first, yourself!"
    Rhynda Stephens, Girls Inc. of Santa Fe

"Dr. Jeanette leads us to create wholeness through sharing courageously how she walked through life's unexpected places. She gives us reason to reflect on the interchange of her experiences with ours. As women, we are known survivors whose strength, tenacity, and creativity carry us through many a storm. This book offers reflections and actions that take one to the depth of the soul while celebrating a woman's power to claim her life as catalyst to thrive, change herself, and change the world."
    Marsie Silvestro, author of *Feast of Sisterly Trance Formation, Grief Walks through Me Like a Rake,* and *The Sky Is My Ocean*

THE PARADOXICAL RETURN OF THE FEMININE

Journeys to Raise Awareness and Create Peace

JEANNETTE M. GAGAN, PHD

Copyright © 2020 by Jeannette M. Gagan, PhD.

All rights reserved. No part of this publication may be reproduced, distributed, or transmitted in any form or by any means, including photocopying, recording, or other electronic or mechanical methods, without the prior written permission of the publisher, except in the case of brief quotations embodied in critical reviews and certain other noncommercial uses permitted by copyright law. For permission requests, write to the publisher, addressed "Attention: Permissions Coordinator," at the address below.

ARPress
45 Dan Road Suite 5
Canton MA 02021

Hotline: 1(800) 220-7660
Fax: 1(855) 752-6001

Ordering Information:
Quantity sales. Special discounts are available on quantity purchases by corporations, associations, and others. For details, contact the publisher at the address above.

Printed in the United States of America.

ISBN-13:	Paperback	979-8-89389-857-6
	Hardcover	979-8-89389-858-3
	eBook	979-8-89389-859-0

Library of Congress Control Number: 2024923850

Contents

Preface vii

Chapter 1. Of Ants and Spiders: Understanding
                Feminine Energy 1
                The Fall of the Female 3
                My Journey: Childhood 9

Chapter 2. My Journey Continues Into Adulthood 14
                Breakthrough 17
                Second Sabbatical 20

Chapter 3. Healing Modalities 25
                Brain Dynamics 25
                Meditation with OECF and FACE 26
                Channeling 27
                Confluence of Knowledge 29

Chapter 4. Restoring the Feminine 36
                The Role of Mother Mary: Perspectives of
                    Balance and Imbalance 39
                Facing One's Shadow Self 42
                Returning to Oneself 45

Chapter 5. Characteristics of a Goddess 53
                Confidence 53
                Doing It All 54
                Speaking Truth 55
                Partnership 56
                Living Goddesses 56

Chapter 6. Ways To Welcome One's Goddess 64
    Therapy 64
    Self-help 65
    ASCs 68
    Shamanism 69
    Non-scientific Trees of Knowledge 71
    What's for You? 86

Chapter 7. Mentors And Non-Mentors 89
    Mentors 92

Chapter 8. Feminine Energy in Relationships 105
    The Seven Principles of Marriage 105
    The Esoteric Path of Marriage 111
    How Relationships Developed in My Life 114

Chapter 9. Sacred Sexuality 120
    Tantra 123
    Meditative Practices That Enhance Sex 132

Chapter 10. The Eternal Goddess 140
    Ho'oponopono 143
    Final Words on Feminine and Masculine Balance 148

Bibliography 155
About the Author 159

Preface

HAVE NO DOUBT: peace is an attainable objective, based in reality, substantiated through history and by the personal experiences of many. Yet we live in a world that seems on a downward spiral of hatred and violence. So how is humankind to create peace: between nations, among all people, within oneself? I believe the answer lies in the link between spirituality and psychology—our first paradox—for in this special juncture can be found the power to nurture and heal.

Precisely what this means will be explained. For now, at the beginning of this journey together, hold in mind that even though my title seems to be a call to the feminine, I am writing for and to both males and females—our second paradox. A basic principle of this book is that the feminine and masculine must be balanced: one must not diminish the other. If such were the case, it would be a repetition of failures of the past.

Being eighty years old, having traveled numerous landscapes of experience where I met countless varieties of people, I understand that life is about challenge and change. While not always welcome, these nonetheless are the key ingredients that provide opportunities for growth, and my life's work has become about raising awareness to these auspicious moments for fulfilling one's true potential.

What I've learned dates back to the end of the Great Depression in the 1930s, at a time when telephones were a novelty and listening to a radio was a prime entertainment, rivaled only by the pleasure of attending Sunday movie matinees. The advent of television after World War II was a marvel to behold and at first was not affordable to many people. Few anticipated how those boxes would permeate our lives. Similarly, in the 1980s when I was in graduate school and introduced to a computer, I had no idea how it would eventually be a mainstay in my work, because at that time computers were used in scientific and commercial ways, with little evidence of eventual evolution into devices for personal and social transactions.

Technology, though, is secondary to what I've gained spiritually and psychologically. Early in my life I had a spiritual bent, which over time intersected with my study of psychology. I have devoted countless hours to investigating where and how these two are aligned. This is my third book on the subject. Psychology, of course, studies among other things the ego, which many see as antithetical to spiritual growth. This is far from true, and by the time you finish reading this book, I think you will agree.

To understand human consciousness, one must ponder the entire picture from a holistic perspective: all systems and their properties—whether economic, physical, biological, social, mental, emotional, psychological, or spiritual—are viewed as wholes and not as a mere collection of parts. In other words, functioning cannot be fully understood by deconstructing and analyzing the component parts. For example, emotions and feelings are considered to be mental representations, but they also have physical and spiritual aspects. When one feels hatred, especially if it is not handled correctly, it can erupt into violence against oneself or others. Worse, if one feels hatred and denies or represses it, that feeling is *more likely* to emerge through harmful acts.

How does spirituality play a crucial role? The path of spirituality is that of acceptance and peace, and it too is innate in each of us. If we can accept that emotions are part of being human and are natural occurrences, we can allow them to be what they are, without judgment. When we cultivate this spiritual way of listening to our internal messages—our internal wisdom—we have access to a guidance system that helps us live a more holistic life. This results in behaviors and attitudes that do not cause harm to ourselves or others and opens our hearts to love ourselves and others. Doing this fully entails becoming aware of and addressing the shadow side of ourselves: our hidden fears, buried desires, or quite simply the lost spiritual path that we all need to navigate our complex world.

As these words are being written, the world is plagued by terrorism, where killing and maiming other human beings is considered justified. Countering such acts are communities that promote peace, made up of individuals who know that the innate and spiritual route is that of peace—whether they follow Islamic, Christian, Mormon, Buddhist, or other faiths and beliefs.

Exploring the spiritual-psychological connection involves a myriad of factors, and we have at our disposal both scientific and non-scientific tools. One of the most powerful of these is shamanism, the oldest healing tradition known to mankind. Across eons of time, the shamanic imprint has deepened, and humanity need only awaken to its wisdom. Shamanic "journeying" involves a meditative state where the shaman communicates with other realms to obtain power and information to heal those entrusted to his or her care. This "soulful" approach addresses the polarity of our natures, and I will write about it in the chapters to come. I have also written about it in my first book, *Journeying: Where Shamanism and Psychology Meet*.

Yes, when we *know* what we want to achieve, we often discover *feelings* arising within us, such as fear, doubt, anger, impatience, and frustration that obstruct our pursuits. We feel conflict within ourselves. However, from a soulful perspective warmed by the alchemical matrix of shamanic practices, the angst of the individual—and of the world—can be contained and transformed. This is an approach that has just begun to be recognized as containing pragmatic, grounded, and scientific aspects, and it is a cornerstone of what I want to share.

In summary, to resolve hatred and violence, we need the return of the feminine—and the return of the feminine requires better understanding of both spirituality and psychology. Paradoxically, this is a call to men as well as women, to mankind as well as womankind.

Each will walk this path in their own way. My own path will be shared in these chapters, as I believe that my experiences may help you explore new areas. In addition to shamanism, which was of great importance in helping me find direction, there are many paradigms that promote the evolution of human awareness, some of which are presented in this book. I offer you a grab basket of such information, to choose those with which you resonate. You are free to read portions of the book that interest and speak to you, while you are also free to skip content that holds no attraction. With these factors in mind, I welcome you to *The Paradoxical Return of the Feminine*, with the belief you will discover information that will empower you in your pursuit of well-being and happiness—which will benefit all of humankind.

Jeannette M. Gagan
Santa Fe, 2017

Chapter 1

Of Ants and Spiders: Understanding Feminine Energy

I HAVE LEARNED SOMETHING from the ants and spiders that frequent my home, each of which has a different lifestyle that illuminates something about we humans and about the feminine energy that both males and females possess. Just as ants and spiders—both male and female—represent feminine energy, humans also—both male and female—embody and can express feminine energy.

Ants favor sweet droppings on the kitchen floor, while spiders spin beautiful webs around doorways. From my purview, they live a carefree and enchanted existence, unburdened by worries about who pays the rent or whether females or males are superior. Ants are social, and much of their activity centers on community endeavors. Skilled architects, they build complex homes, galleries, and even vaulted ceilings. From the perspective of shamanism, because they live in the earth they represent the ability to ground oneself and to work collaboratively for the common good. They participate in food exchanges as well as gathering, hunting, and growing. Moreover, they share a common goal that ultimately serves the queen. A queen ant has wings and the ability to fly until her eggs are fertilized. Once fertilized, she pulls off her wings and sacrifices her own flight for the birth of the newborn and for the future of the whole colony.

Spiders, on the other hand, spend much of their lives alone, spinning isolated webs that also are architectural marvels. The spider within its web reflects the quiet center of one's own world, which humans access through meditative knowing of oneself and thus knowing the universe. Spiders symbolize mysticism and demonstrate how to maintain balance between the past and the future. Because of their webs, they also signify the magic of creation, linked to feminine energy. Many cultures associate spiders with keeping feminine energy alive and strong.

Like ants, humans sometimes have social aims, with roles more or less defined by the collective goal. At other times, we need solitude for our creative undertakings and to be the weavers of our own destiny. Each of these creatures reflect aspects of feminine energy that are important attributes for males and females to cultivate within themselves, as they are crucial elements in achieving peace in the world. Feminine energy, then, concerns: grounding oneself, social relatedness, nurturing self and others, creativity, and self-knowledge.

Increasingly we hear from caring and thoughtful people: *it will be women who save the world*. One needs only to listen to the morning news to know how violence, hatred, and destruction threaten this planet. As I write this, the United States is grappling with a seemingly endless and escalating series of race-based killings that highlight how our nation carries the psychological imprint of prejudice and hatred toward people of different races and skin colors. We can also add to this list violence against gays, immigrants, and even our planet, through the destruction of natural resources.

There is no question that healing and restoration need to happen individually, interpersonally, and culturally. We will need the lessons of ants and spiders to bring about change. We will need to rally *the feminine energy that resides in us all* to heal the planet's wounds. Women can and will be the leaders who save the world because they are more in touch with—and generally more accepting of—their feelings, which is a core ingredient to improving the world, as will be elaborated.

I want to be clear, however: there is a key distinction between *female energy* and *feminine energy*. **Female energy** is based on the physical differences between males and females, such as wider hips, broader faces, menstruating, becoming pregnant, and lactating (while men are larger and stronger, have more body hair, and live shorter lives). **Feminine energy** connotes psychological and spiritual perspectives that men also possess and can exercise, as is seen when they nurture children, express their emotions, hone their intuition, and inhabit the world in a more globally holistic way.

Males indeed can join hands with females and be leaders who balance the world—and it won't be for the first time.

The Fall of the Female

We know that women once enjoyed more status and power in some ancient cultures than they generally do today. Inanna was a prominent female deity in ancient Mesopotamia around 3100 BCE. A famous vase shows a row of naked men bringing various objects to her. Associated with the planet Venus, she is said to represent a dual nature as the goddess of love and war, with both masculine and feminine qualities. At our present time in history—since she embodies traits of independence, self-determination, and strength within the patriarchal Sumerian pantheon—she is a subject of feminist theory and regarded by some as the mother of all humanity. Interestingly, archaeologist and historian Anne O Nomis (2006) describes Inanna's rituals as including some emotionally charged aspects "imbued with pain and ecstasy, bringing about initiation and journeys of altered consciousness; punishment, ecstasy, lament, and song; participants exhausting themselves with weeping and grief" (Nomis, 2006, pp. 59-60).

Similarly, *In Search of the Lost Feminine* author Craig S. Barnes (2006) traces historical events of the last three millennia, when patriarchal rule dominated. Hallmarks include craving for and manipulation of power, valuing knowledge over intuition, and seeking influence over death, with conceivable immortality achieved through military heroism. On the other hand, prior to 1500 BCE, the Minoan culture (as demonstrated by archeological findings and discovery of artifacts found on the island of Crete) portrayed a more beneficial and *peaceful* society. Absent from Minoan archaeology are themes emphasizing male domination of females. There is no depiction of men presiding over or subduing women; there are no paintings of spears and swords or graphic scenes of violence between humans; and in thousands of images there is not one that shows brutality to women.

Women were honored in art and are shown to be wearing embroidered dresses, flowers in their hair, and splendid necklaces. Sensuality was no stranger to these females, since among the unearthed articles were found depictions of women with dresses open in the front, exposing their breasts. Spirituality was also a given in this culture, as there is significant evidence the "Minoans went to the mountains to pray, to throw their arms upward in exaltation to dance, to swirl and swing under the moon" (Barnes, 2006, p. 19). Furthermore, a woman was considered to be embedded within a cycle that regenerates life from death—a perspective that involves endless rebirth, with immortality a natural consequence, incomprehensible as that may seem to many individuals.

What occurred between the decline of the Minoan civilization and our present time involved what Barnes terms the "fall of the female," evidenced in numerous ways. Suppression of women along with their submission to men became standard. A tragic, graphic example of patriarchal exploits was that of burning at the stake so-called witches—estimated to be from seventy thousand to millions throughout the centuries.

Women like Joan [of Arc] who acted with unusual independence and power—midwives, healers, women who drove hard bargains in the sale of eggs or a cow, women whose husbands were impotent, women who were themselves barren—were through the course of the period charged as witches (Barnes, 2006, p. 221).

This trend is by no means dead. Though burning at the stake is rare, abuse of females is evident across the globe. Religious doctrine typically forms the foundation of such misogynistic practices. Hatred of women can be documented in the texts of many of the world's chief religions. Currently, increasing attention is being given to the plight of females living in some Muslim countries, such as Saudi Arabia, Sudan, and Iran, where women are subjugated under extremist interpretations of *Shariah* law, which is considered the infallible law of God. The origin of this law rests in the Qur'an and in the traditions of the Islamic prophet Muhammad, who was born around 570 CE and, in his adulthood, caused a revolution that altered the course of history.

The legacy of Muhammad carries a universal message that includes the values of justice, freedom, fraternity, charity, and equality. Nonetheless, variations and misinterpretations increasingly overshadow the purity of these teachings. Introduction of tainted aspects of Shariah globally is an established goal for militant Islamists, and their indoctrination now infiltrates many countries, including those in the West. Believers often act out in violence, murder, and even warfare. The perverse teachings involve totalitarian, discriminatory practices that wage war on women and result in a form of gender "apartheid." Females become second-class citizens who are considered property of their husbands and families. Honor killings, spousal abuse, and female genital mutilation of girls are just some of the atrocities. Girls—sometimes as young as nine years old—are forced into marriage, and many undergo early childbirth with high maternal death rates. A female seeking education or freedom may be beaten, burned with acid or fire, or imprisoned.

Undeniably, there are serious perils and challenges to being a female on this planet. Whether a woman lives in the United States, Japan, India, or elsewhere, to one degree or another, it is apparent females have yet to gain equal footing with males.

In the United States, we have seen some progress within the last century, particularly in the political arena: women have advanced from not being allowed to vote, let alone serve as a legislator, to being an important electorate and holding public office. In fact, the 2012 elections resulted in a record number of 101 females serving in the House of Representatives, followed by a decline in the 2014 elections to a number of 84. In the US Senate, both the 2012 and 2014 elections resulted in a total of 20 females being elected. As a result of the 2016 elections, when the 115th Congress convenes in 2017, there will be 83 women in the House of Representatives (a decrease of one) and 21 women in the Senate (an increase of one). This brings the total of women in Congress to 104, which is the same as in 2014 election—unfortunately showing a lack of progress.

Notably the aftermath of the 2016 election has been one of volatility. Many females have engaged in marches and demonstrations in protest of results. From a broader perspective it is imperative that feminine energy comes together in a positive way—not focusing on blame, delineating constructive solutions to problems, and uniting in strength to resolve them. More about such movements will be detailed in later chapters.

Elsewhere, women are not only functioning as CEOs of corporations and being in command of national and state government agencies, they also are increasingly established as physicians, dentists, and lawyers, to name just a few professional fields. In the November 2016 election, the woman nominated as a presidential candidate by a major party for the first time in US history did not win the election. Even so, this is a major step forward for women worldwide. In fact, the aftermath of this election has drawn that much more attention to the need for female leadership.

The news is not as bright regarding wage differences between male and female employees. Although studies focusing on wage differences indicate discrepancies, they all indicate lower wages for women as compared to men, and women of color fare worse than white women. Even more educated women were paid less than their male peers. According to the American Association of University Women (2013), in 2012 among full-time, year- round workers, women were paid 77 percent of what men were paid in nearly every occupation—the same as 2002. And racially, African American women were paid 64 percent and Hispanic women were paid 53 percent of what a white man earns.

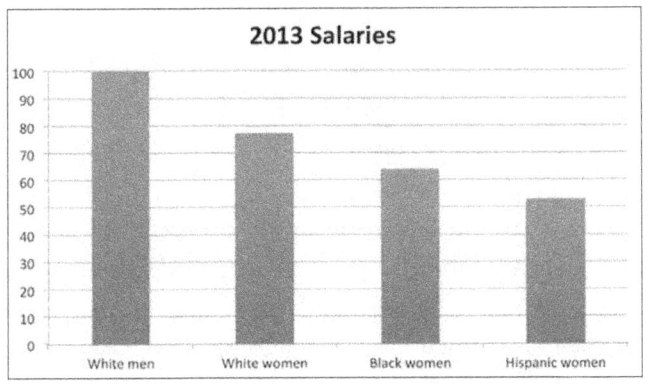

Source: **American Association of University Women**

The Bureau of Labor Statistics indicates similar differences. Of note, in 2012 Asian women earned more than their white, black, and Hispanic counterparts. The first report published by the Bureau of Labor Statistics on wages was published in 1979, which indicated women earned 62 percent of what men earned. Obviously, increases in women's wages over this thirty- six-year period are substantial, and we can hope that the trend will continue until there is parity.

Sheryl Sandberg, author of *Lean In: Women, Work, and the Will to Lead* (2014), provides detailed information regarding the inequalities between male and female, including salaries, types of available jobs, and stereotypical attitudes toward women. She also presents data regarding how very few women are in presidential positions in the independent countries in the world and even fewer functioning as CEOs of the Fortune 500. Importantly, her book provides specific targets for women to address on their path to equality:

- underestimating oneself;
- dealing with successful women being liked less;

- embracing the importance of mentorship;
- seeking and speaking the truth;
- creating a true partnership;
- dealing with the myth of doing it all; and
- working together toward equality.

Sandberg emphasizes how more women in leadership roles benefits business and society, and she encourages women (whose life circumstances and personal preferences allow them to do so) to vigorously pursue any career goal.

US gender disparities are recognized outside our borders, as well. A year after Sandberg's book was published, three women from Poland, the United Kingdom, and Costa Rica visited the United States in 2015 as part of a United Nations human rights delegation. Specifically, they assessed discrimination against women and gender inequality. Over the course of ten days, they visited Alabama, Texas, and Oregon to evaluate policies and attitudes, as well as school, health, and prison systems. They were horrified by the lack of gender equality in America and found this country to be lagging far behind international human rights standards in a number of areas: a 23 percent gender pay gap, lack of maternity leave, lack of affordable child care, and harsh treatment of female immigrants in detention centers. When they visited an Alabama abortion clinic, they experienced firsthand the hostility of opponents to women's reproductive rights. Even though each woman in the delegation was past childbearing age, they were harassed by two vigilante men. Violence against women was another area of significance, since women in the U.S. are eleven times more likely to be killed by a gun than any other high-income country.

Perhaps the delegation's biggest surprise was discovering that women in the U.S. don't seem to know what they're missing. The problem is that many people believe American women are much better off regarding rights than other women in the world. However, the United States is one of three countries that does not provide women paid maternity leave. Surprisingly, there is little organized protest about it. Recommendations made by the delegation include federal gun restrictions; campaign finance reform (since men dominate and control most money raised for political candidacies) so more women are elected to office; and raising the minimum wage, which disproportionately affects women.

My Journey: Childhood

Females in many present-day cultures experience misogyny on both social and personal levels, and many societies try to hide or deny the abuses. Nonetheless, more and more individuals are bravely, candidly sharing the truth of violations they endured, thereby helping to expose the harms and heal the wounds—and, hopefully, reduce their occurrence. I stand with these women. As the famous saying goes: if we cannot remember our history, we will repeat it. To which I would add: If we cannot become aware of our emotions, we cannot grow. If we cannot talk about our injuries, we cannot effect change.

I was born in 1936, into a Catholic family in the Midwest. All four of my grandparents were of German descent, and they transmitted a distinctly chauvinistic heritage, augmented by Catholicism. My mother was expected to "obey" her husband, which meant she rarely disagreed with him openly. He worked outside the home, while she stayed home and took care of the children. My father pronounced the rules as to how things were to be, and my mother and we children followed them. I don't remember my parents talking much to each other or going places together—they maintained distant, very separate lives. At the time, I experienced this as "normal"; almost every family I knew functioned similarly. I saw no evidence of couples working together to create a true partnership.

The rigid family structure was hard on me, too. Little was known in those days about healthy attachments between parents and children—strictness was both the rule and remedy applied to any problem. One of my father's favorite stories involved a carpenter who, while working on the house, reported that an infant (me) had been crying in the bedroom for a long time. My father replied, "That's how we raise our children—by not spoiling or coddling them." Today, of course, it is more broadly understood that children need holding as well as to be protected from overstimulation. Even more troubling for me was that my mother—already burdened by five children—was emotionally drained and unable to adequately bond with me.

Through the work I have done to understand my earliest days of existence, I have become aware of the persistent loneliness I experienced. I didn't feel close to my mother, my father, or my siblings. I also kept a tight lid on my emotions—so tight, in fact, that throughout my childhood I carried no conscious memory of the sexual abuse I endured, perpetrated by several male relatives. Not until my adult years did dreams and memories surface, leading me back to that trauma.

Another vivid example of my repression of emotions concerns my mother's death. Shortly after the birth of her seventh child, when I was five, she was diagnosed with cancer. She died three years later, when I was eight. As her casket was lowered into the grave, I remember others around me crying. Yet I did not feel sadness but a strong awareness that it was *she* who had died—*I* was alive and would not give in to weeping and would focus on living my life in a vibrant way.

What actually was occurring within me was denial of the reality of her death, denial of the tremendous pain I felt in not having bonded with her, and denial of the rage I felt about her inability to protect me from sexual abuse (which I now believe she did not know was occurring). This degree of denial is, of course, an unconscious process, and it would present obstacles for my ongoing development; nevertheless, as with many other attempts to cope, it was necessary for me to survive emotionally. It would be decades before I could risk seeking and speaking my truth.

As is true for all types of repression, what is stuffed in the unconscious finds expression through other means, typically disguised so that one does not recognize them. After my mother's death, I entered a period of intense adoration of the Blessed Virgin Mary. Daily, no matter the weather, I walked the four blocks to St. Mary's Church and knelt in the dim shadows at the side altar where Mary's outstretched hands signaled comfort and possibility. Having been told the story of Fatima, wherein three Portuguese children tending sheep experienced an apparition of the Blessed Virgin, I secretly hoped for such an encounter. I felt like a lost sheep and yearned for a mother replacement. But my missions were futile: she remained a statue, and my sense of disconnection prevailed.

In fact, the Catholic religion imposed many complications on my developing psyche. By this time, I had made my first confession and received my first Holy Communion. While these rituals are intended to lead to salvation, the real-time effect is that I felt and believed I was a sinner. Going regularly to confess sins became a matter of intense confusion. Telling the priest that "I was angry five times" didn't make much sense, for I knew the next week I would return with the same "sin" to confess. This is an early example of how I, like so many others, was trained to deplore my emotions instead of explore and accept them.

As I became an adolescent, this problem was confounded by confessing, "every day I have many bad thoughts"—that is, sexual in nature. All of which resulted in me becoming scrupulous, as I painstakingly worried about what was a sin and what was not. Helplessly I tried to sort through feelings of anger, sexuality, truthfulness, and selfishness. Finding no answers but driven to understand, I scrutinized my every thought and feeling. Psychologically speaking, such concern is described as *obsessive compulsiveness*: a trait that is difficult to control although, in the long run, as you will later see, this tendency has a flip side that served me well. Spiritually speaking, there was also a dividend to my scruples:

I became certain there *was* a spiritual reality to myself and to life, even though I did not know how to tap into it.

In summation, this chapter details various female challenges—cultural, social, political, emotional, and spiritual—and offers a glimpse of how, in certain areas, this is changing and will continue to do so, hopefully at a quickened pace. My sharing of events earlier in my life illustrates how change happened for me as an individual and, as you will read in coming chapters, continues to occur. A major reason for writing this book is to share these experiences to inspire readers to commit to needed changes that will foster development of a more emotionally and spiritually fulfilling life.

WORKS CITED

American Association of Professional Women (September 13,2013). "The simple truth about the gender pay gap." Retrieved from http://aauw.org/research/thesimple-truth -about-the-gender-pay-gap/ Barnes, C. (2006). *In search of the lost feminine*. Golden, CO: Fulcrum Publishing.

Ibid., 19.

Ibid., 221.

Muhammad information retrieved from http:///www.inspiredbymuhammad.com/muhammad.php?&content_76=3 and http://en.wikipedia.org/wiki/Sharia and http://the shariahwaronwomen.org.about

Nomis, A. (2013). "A Hymn to Inanna (Inanna C)." *The electronic text corpus of Sumerian literature*, lines 70-80, cited in Anne O Nomis, *Dominiatrix rituals of gender, transformation, ecstasy and pain* (pp. 59-60).

Sandburg, S. (2014). *Lean in: Women, work, and the will to lead.* New York: Alfred A. Knopf.

Shariah information retrieved from http://en.wikipedia.org/wiki/Sharia and http://theshariahwaronwomen.org.about and http://www.inspiredbymuhammad.com/muhammad.php?&content_76=3

U.S. Bureau of Labor Statistics (October 2013). "Highlights of women's earnings in 2012" retrieved from www.bls.gov

U.S. Bureau of Labor Statistics (2015). USDL-15-0688: "Usual weekly earnings of wage and salary workers: first quarter 2015" retrieved from www.bls.gov

Chapter 2

My Journey Continues Into Adulthood

ONE OF THE marvels of all living things is that the life force carries us through devastating setbacks. Ants and spiders can have limbs torn off and still participate in their respective activities. Likewise, many humans have rocky beginnings and end up living fulfilling adulthoods. Fortunately, so did I.

With the hormonal changes of adolescence, my attention to personal scruples broadened and turned to other matters. I was a good student, blessed with adequate intelligence. In high school, in addition to making straight-A grades and being the valedictorian of my graduating class, I worked in a doctor's office on evenings and weekends. My goal was to attend college and obtain a Bachelor of Science degree in nursing. To this end, my oldest sister, with whom I had the closest relationship of all my siblings, convinced me to attend Marquette University in Milwaukee, Wisconsin, where she and her husband lived. This was a fortuitous choice, as I discovered the Jesuit priests of this university had a more expansive view and understanding of Catholicism. After having several counseling sessions with one of the Jesuits, I understood how my scruples were a hindrance to my full emotional growth, and I was able to lessen their intensity.

A new era of my life began after graduating and working for a year as a nurse: I married and had children. Remembering the distance between my parents, I had hoped to find a man who would be more communicative and enjoy doing things with me. Fortunately, I found such a man. My husband graduated from Marquette with a medical degree, and we settled in a small town where he served as a family practitioner. During these happy and gratifying years, I gave birth to five children.

Even though I took seriously my marriage vow of loving and obeying my husband, the cultural perspectives in this country were undergoing tremendous change—the phenomena of the 1960s and 1970s could not be ignored, especially feminism. I became more confident about speaking my mind, and I became a civil rights activist. At one point, my husband and I considered moving to a country in Africa where my husband would work in a medical clinic. But when I was told I would serve as the Bishop's secretary, we reconsidered our options; I did not want to be subservient to a Bishop.

Instead we moved to northern New Mexico. We wanted to be involved with a population that was in need of affordable healthcare. Consequently, my husband worked in a small, rural hospital that provided medical treatment at a low fee. Here, living among Hispanic people, we experienced for the first time being the minority. We also were not accustomed to living among people who seemed to be borderline impoverished. The area also was populated by a burgeoning hippie population, which had a great influence on us. Although we did not espouse to be hippies, these two cultural influences led us to question many areas of our way of life, leading to the realization that self-exploration and understanding was to be our top priority. Consequently, we packed up our belongings and the entire family traveled in a van with a small trailer for six months.

A time of reflection and review of our lives ensued. Our "time out" allowed us to read and discuss spiritual and philosophical books that deepened our self-awareness and offered each of us the opportunity to assess how we would proceed in our lives. We knew we didn't want to return to the Midwest, as northern New Mexico is rich with cultural diversity and spiritual influences.

When we returned to New Mexico and asked our children—ages five to eleven—if they were ready to return to school, four of them said yes and the fifth said he would go along with sibling consensus. I asked my husband what he wanted to do professionally and/or creatively, and he made the decision to become an emergency-room physician. Noticing that no one asked *me* what I wanted to do, I felt disappointed and upset. I was very willing to return to work as a nurse, but that was not to be; I was to be a homemaker. At that point, neither my husband nor I were able to work together toward equality and to create a true partnership.

As you have guessed by now, I had crossed a threshold that forever changed my life and my way of being and thinking. By this time, we were no longer Catholics, and I no longer believed in "obeying" my husband. I wanted to listen to his views, and then I wanted him to listen to my views, so that together we could negotiate an outcome. But this did not occur. For a number of years, I stewed in my juices, as the quality of our marriage relationship deteriorated.

When I eventually decided to pursue a master's degree in mental health nursing, my husband was agreeable upon the condition that I continue to care for our children and the house in the way that I always had, to which I agreed. After I completed the degree and obtained a part-time job, I announced I was applying for admission to a full-time doctoral program in counseling psychology. I completed that program within three years, by which time my husband had reconciled himself to the reality of my new profession and that things at home could not remain frozen in time. He had always respected my intelligence and began to think in terms of how I could work full-time, as our children were now leaving home.

Of course, my personality could not remain frozen in time, either. Throughout these years of education, I also worked long and hard on troublesome aspects of my past. The emotional deficits and spiritual confusion that overshadowed my growing-up years were becoming more conscious. I realized that, just as my childhood had not been able to support the emergence of my vital self, neither had my marriage. The root of our marriage problem remained, as we had not learned how to deal with emotional difficulties between us—in other words, our egos were not mature enough to handle the distressing situations that routinely occur in marriage.

We were not alone in our plight, as the divorce rate in this country was spiraling upward. We didn't divorce then, but in 1987 I moved into separate living quarters, initiating a time of marital separation that lasted until 1991. During that time, I established a full-time psychology practice. However, I never stopped loving this man and hoped against hope we would reconcile and begin a new type of partnership. We did consider this, but unfortunately the attempt fizzled. In 1991 I filed for divorce, and when the legal papers were signed, we agreed to remain friends and not to criticize each other in the presence of our children. This agreement stands to this day, for which I am most grateful. Fortunately we were able to forge a longstanding friendship.

These changes, both difficult and beneficial, came with many questions and challenging feelings. Uppermost: Why, after all the psychological work I had done, was I feeling a despair that seemed to extend back in my life to long before the ending of my marriage? What had happened to me, other than incidents I held in conscious memory? I had an intuition that buried traumas were pressing for conscious acknowledgment.

Breakthrough

I took a sabbatical from my psychology practice and moved to the country. This was a spider time, during which I lived in an isolated place and weaved past experiences with a more mystical future—a future that I believed would be more in accord with my spiritual self.

What occurred throughout those eighteen months of the sabbatical, I described in the prologue of my first book, published in 1998, entitled *Journeying: Where Shamanism and Psychology Meet*. Without going into minute detail and to avoid repetition of

Journeying content, a condensed account of these months is that realizations surfaced of the sexual and emotional abuse I experienced in childhood. Fortunately, this resulted in my discovery of the instrumental role of shamanism in the healing of such wounds.

My interest in shamanic phenomena first occurred during graduate school, when I had taken a number of courses in cross-cultural psychology. At the same time, I was receiving training in Ericksonian hypnosis. Having discovered in my reading that trance states were natural occurrences in many cultures and that they could induce psychological healing, I began to read books on shamanism, attended trainings sponsored by the Foundation for Shamanic Studies, and engaged in an intensive teaching from Twylah Nitsch, a Seneca elder. Learning how to journey—that is, entering a shamanic trance—involves traveling to the Lower World and encountering power animals and spirit beings who not only protected and nurtured me but also showed me ways to heal. Very specifically and of most relevance, this included learning how to acknowledge the repressed rage from childhood abuse and to release it within the safety and containment of the journeying domain. In so doing, I came to understand how the energy of such release is transformed for use in other healing endeavors.

In twenty-one years of consciously struggling to resolve my psychological dilemmas, I had utilized many approaches—from traditional verbal therapy to consciousness-raising workshops, and from hypnosis and imagery to psychodrama—none of which afforded the healing power I experienced in the shamanic realm. The underlying depressive tenor to my existence then gave way to an appreciation of life; waking in the morning was not shrouded in silent dread of how loneliness and disconnection would play themselves out in the day before me. The belief that recurrent loss would dominate my life was displaced by contentment in relating with my children, grandchildren, and friends.

When I returned to my psychotherapy practice, I selectively incorporated shamanic approaches into my clinical work. All the while I was mesmerized by questions that engaged my analytical mind: How does the shamanic tradition bring such potent healing power to wounds incurred in the earliest months of life? Beyond individual gains, could journeying provide a release valve for the violence so rampant in our world?

I hoped to find answers to the first question by examining the philosophical, historical, and methodological underpinnings of shamanism and psychology. The second question evoked fascination and more questions. Coming to terms with my own capacity for violent expression had sharpened my view of public displays of hostility. Aggression, I realized, deepens its imprint on our consciousness each time we see hatred in the eyes of a passing stranger or witness abuse heaped on a child in the marketplace. This imprint reminds us of our own aggressive thoughts and impulses, and if we haven't come to terms with this, there is fear as well as lack of knowing how to deal with such emotions when they surface. No longer is the propensity for violence relegated to the delinquent few, or even to an "unspeakable" tendency peeking out from closets of the privileged and protected. *Countless* world citizens have grown up with the breath of violence hot and sultry on their necks. In the United States, descriptions of violent events too often dominate reports of national news. Undeniably, the number of homicides committed by juveniles confounds our notion of childhood.

How is it possible to "turn the other cheek," I wondered, when there is no immunity against the epidemic of street and family violence? What does it mean to "do unto others as you would have them do to unto you," when basic rights to live have not been granted? What are the prospects for four-year- olds who fear nuclear obliteration, worry about chemical crippling, or watch older siblings tote guns to schools?

As I studied books on the subject, a theoretical bridge emerged, linking early developmental wounding with shamanic healing: beings encountered in shamanic journeys have the potential to fill the void left by developmental deprivation. Between the realms of shamanism and psychology, I saw a methodological meeting place rich with implications for redressing acting-out behaviors, blaming others, extreme loneliness, depression, and confusion— along with the physical ailments that sometimes accompany such emotional disruptions. The *Journeying* book is the result of my explorations. This was an expansive time in my life, during which I felt a sense of accomplishment and deepened purpose. From another perspective, it was an "ant time" of being social and orchestrating a new life that involved community and teaching endeavors.

Second Sabbatical

My first sabbatical had been transformative, but my journey had twists and turns yet to come. In the late 1990s, when I began to write my second book, *Grow Up Your Ego*, I delved intensively into research about the relationship between parents and infant—results that troubled me. Deeper awareness came when a psychologist trained in Ericksonian hypnotherapy did a session with me. While in a trance state, I experienced being in the home of my mother's growing-up years. To my surprise, an elephant was trying to climb the stairs from the basement to the main floor. When the therapist and I discussed this, I remarked on the common expression of *an elephant in the room*—i.e., the huge thing that everyone ignores. I then understood I had been ignoring the "elephant" in my past: the dysfunctional relationship with my mother.

As many readers know, such realizations may break through in a specific, sudden moment, but they absorb a great deal of subsequent time and emotional struggle if one chooses to work through them. I chose to experience the feelings that arose—and the emotional fallout was far more intense than I anticipated.

By the beginning of 2003 I knew something major—and disruptive—was occurring. I awoke with dread, was tired all day, and felt depressed. I closed my psychology practice in June of that year and began another sabbatical— another spider time of isolation and inward focus—a time I assumed would last a year or two at the most.

I began to experience immense anxiety that resulted in seeing a psychiatrist, who prescribed antidepressants. This, however, only increased my anxiety (for some patients, one side effect of antidepressants is anxiety). I stopped taking the medication. Having been diagnosed with PTSD (Post Traumatic Stress Disorder, a common result of sexual abuse), I was then prescribed Ativan—a drug that reduces anxiety. I was reluctant to take it but agreed to a low dosage, which helped me navigate through daily tasks such as cooking and doing physical exercise. Fortunately, as I began to heal, I was able to wean myself off Ativan—a feat that helped me feel better, as it increased my self-confidence to completely restore myself to health In the early days of this experience friends, colleagues, and family members were supportive and came by frequently. Nonetheless, as time passed and my emotional state did not improve, their visits dwindled, and I felt interest in me and my welfare had worn thin. Furthermore, I felt shame regarding my inability to heal myself—"the expert," so to speak, on shamanic and psychological healing techniques. In many ways, I felt relief as contact with others diminished.

About this time, I entered counseling with an experienced and wise psychotherapist, with whom I had sessions until the end of 2012. Our work focused on faulty bonding issues in addition to memories that emerged regarding sexual abuse far beyond what I had realized during my first sabbatical. As shocking as this was, it gave me insight into the role anxiety plays when a person is dealing with long-repressed abusive events. By the end of 2012, I understood that I hadn't been ready or strong enough in my previous sabbatical to take on the reality of the extent of the sexual abuse. It was as though the first sabbatical was a preparatory exercise for the second.

I share these details not to bemoan my childhood but to assure readers that it is common for memories to be layered like this; awareness of an upper layer often leads to deeper and earlier memories.

Do not fear this part of your journey—it is not a bottomless well or a sinking boat or any other analogy of hopelessness. The good news is that there are many healing modalities, and I will be exploring those in more detail in Chapter 3.

The strong focus of this time of reflection covers many chapters. Perhaps the most outstanding feature was my loneliness and isolation. Prior to my breakdown, I interacted a great deal with my children, who by then were married or partnered, and my six grandchildren. I had been their matriarch who took great pleasure in spending time with them. I was the hostess of family gatherings, cooked yummy food, and promoted the philosophy of "the more the merrier." I was the grandmother who routinely invited grandchildren for special sleepovers they very much enjoyed and looked forward to. I was also an accomplished, talented professional, recognized as an adept shamanic practitioner with a book on the subject to prove it. I could feel my children delight in these achievements and success.

But as months turned into years and it didn't seem I was getting any better or getting on with my life, their dismay and feelings of helplessness regarding my plight led to ever-diminishing interactions. This phenomenon was the most painful of those years. It isn't that they didn't care or didn't love me— they just didn't know what would be of help. Understanding this only deepened my shame, as I realized how the mother they knew and loved was no longer available to them and perhaps no longer wanted to be close to them. The latter was far from the truth, as I felt deep sadness about missing out on so many years of their lives, especially with my grandchildren, who were growing up so quickly.

I owe a debt of gratitude to my ex-husband, who befriended me in a new way throughout these years. Once a week he would come to visit for several hours. He had physical health problems, and we supported each other through conversation, giving rides to the other when needed, and offering helpful suggestions. I did not, however, share the depth of my healing struggle, as I believed it would have been difficult for him to cope with its complexities, and it was my intent to support his good health, not burden him.

The lack of interaction with friends and family resulted in long days with time hanging heavy on my hands. My anxiety kept me from going to movies, reading books, watching TV, pursuing a hobby, or reaching out to others. I seldom ate at restaurants. Because the anxiety also affected my digestive system, the number of foods I could eat was limited. I expended much effort in cooking and eating what was most tolerable and healthy. This and daily physical exercise—walking in my neighborhood, swimming, and working out on exercise machines—became a lifesaver, as they not only contributed to good health, they also gave me a sense of accomplishment.

My professional background and expertise also were extremely important to me. Throughout these years, I satisfied all necessary requirements for license renewal, including obtaining continuing education credits both for my registered nurse license and psychology license. My doctoral degree from a traditional program had been hard won, and my licensure as a psychologist awarded me credibility in a world I valued.

A final chapter of this decade involves money. Although I had a savings account, money in an IRA, and a small inheritance from a relative, I needed a sizable income to cover my mortgage and to pay for therapy sessions and living expenses. Each year there was a substantial depletion of my savings. By 2007 I sold my house, which had a home office, paid off the mortgage, and downsized to a townhouse, for which I paid cash. This move took a great deal of stamina to prepare for and to complete. Fortunately family members helped, and I soon settled into an environment where there were walking paths in a friendly neighborhood.

In spite of economic concerns throughout these years, it was an automatic and easy decision to spend many thousands of dollars on the various therapies I engaged in. My goal was to heal, and I would leave no stone unturned to do so, even if it meant becoming a grand

and happy old bag lady in the end! Attending therapy sessions took up considerable time, because I carefully prepared for them and recorded in my journal what occurred, so I could incorporate what I learned to reap the most healing benefit. This is where the upside of obsessive compulsiveness came into play, as my determination to heal was supported by meticulous adherence to what was needed to surmount obstacles.

How does feminine energy pertain to this part of my journey? It is a fact that females are more likely to engage in psychotherapy sessions than males, in part because they listen to their intuition and inner wisdom to know when the time is ripe for their successful emergence into a life of truthful expression. Many psychotherapeutic approaches as well as journeying experiences guide one to such awareness of inner wisdom. These techniques also help females to accept, own, and express their *innate power*, as they learn to become appropriately and confidently assertive in a safe, professional setting.

And finally, exercising one's own feminine energy is contagious: being honest and forthright about one's psychological and spiritual states provides impetus to others to choose their own healing path. I learned this firsthand when I came to terms with my shame about what I perceived as my downfall. No male or female is perfect, and this planet earth is a place of learning, of accepting the value of one's essence, and of having the courage to manifest that truth. The main reason I am writing this book is to show others that no matter your age (I am now in my early eighties) it is never too late to emotionally and spiritually mature.

Chapter 3

Healing Modalities

MY PERSONAL EXPERIENCE with shamanic healing methods, including my study of them and their application, left no doubt in my mind about their efficacy. At the same time, I had developed an interest in and respect for other healing philosophies and practitioners—massage therapists, body workers, and biofeedback therapists, to name a few—that I now want to share, in the hope you will explore those modalities that appeal to you.

At the outset, I want to address an important factor that underpins them all: the quality of the *relationship* between the healer and healee. Some of the practitioners I encountered exhibited judgmental attitudes toward me and my situation, which always resulted in my decision to cease and desist from crossing their thresholds again. I totally endorse and agree with research showing how the *therapeutic relationship* impacts healing and improvement. That is why therapy with the experienced and compassionate psychotherapist was successful and why the two years I was in Brain Dynamics training with a very wise and spiritual psychologist resulted in such positive outcomes.

Brain Dynamics

Brain Dynamics is a sophisticated technique used to assess and improve the functioning of specific parts of the brain. It involves a computer and the placing of electrodes on the client's head as she or he listens to sounds via earphones, simultaneously focusing on keeping the sound either high or low, depending on the specific protocol. The electrodes are moved to various locations on the head as the client actively participates in the process. It is unlike shock treatments used in electro-convulsive therapy, which cause seizures to effect change.

Most people undergo Brain Dynamics for a limited number of sessions. My course of treatment was longer, due to my basic obsessive compulsiveness, which was still somewhat in place, along with my age. It lasted two years, beginning with sessions three times a week that over time gradually reduced to once weekly and then biweekly as improvement occurred. Benefits I received from this modality included no longer being plagued by terror, a healthier digestive system, meditating every day, comfortably interacting with others, preparing to reactivate my psychology practice, enthusiastically promoting my books, and outlining chapters for a third book.

Meditation with OECF and FACE

Approximately eight years into my awareness of my past trauma, when I began Brain Dynamics sessions, the psychologist revealed to me that he meditated daily, during which time he communicated with spiritual beings, whom he referred to as "The Gang" (see below for more information on channeling). The Gang taught him the practice of OECF—a new and innovative way to meditate. As I learned about this, I saw it had much in common with shamanic approaches. It also is akin to author and psychologist Christopher Germer's (2009) **FACE** approach to meditation:

> **F**EEL the feeling;
> **A**CKNOWLEDGE it;
> (Show) **C**OMPASSION toward it;
> **E**XPECT a positive outcome.

Likewise, in the **OECF** application this involves:
  OPEN (to the feeling);
  EXPAND (make it larger);
  CONNECT (to it);
  FOLLOW (allow whatever occurs to unfold).

Both approaches involve learning and experiencing that emotions are neither right nor wrong—they just are. Instead of trying to repress or ignore them, one meets them with openness and acceptance. As simple as that sounds, mastering this furthers change in powerfully constructive ways.

For me, it was a magnificent advancement from what I learned in my childhood about confessing my emotional states to a priest. Paradoxically, what was then judged as "bad" was now experienced in a spiritual and meditative way that transformed energy into positive outcomes. Furthermore, I discovered when using either the FACE or OECF practice that I sometimes entered into journeying terrain, where my power animal and spiritual helpers were immediately available to help in this transformation of emotional energy into a new, spiritually nourishing way of living and being.

Consequently, I begin each day with this practice. Readers wishing more detailed information can refer to Christopher Germer's book, *The Mindful Path to Self Compassion: Freeing Yourself from Destructive Thoughts and Emotions*. Chapter 8, detailing the FACE exercise, is especially helpful, as well as Appendix B that describes additional self-compassion exercises.

Channeling

Returning to the subject of Brain Dynamics, I suspected what was occurring in the psychologist's meditations was the "channeling" of information from beings—such as angels, ascended masters, and teachers—that conveys great healing benefit. Channeling involves the process of communicating with any consciousness that is not in human form by allowing that consciousness to express itself through an individual—the channeler. Historically it has always been part of the human connection to a higher vibration of thought (for more on vibrations, see Numerology in Chapter 6). Even the knowledge in sacred books of major religions was said to be delivered by gods, messiahs, prophets, and angels. In recent years it has become the belief of numerous spiritually attuned individuals that anyone has the ability to channel and receive information from a higher source. However, discernment is required, since a human channeler carries the potential to add his/her agenda to the message or may not be sufficiently mature to dispense spiritual information.

My first exposure to channeled information occurred in the 1980s, when I attended a gathering with a trusted colleague in which one of his acquaintances, Mary-Margaret Moore, channeled information from an entity called Bartholomew (Mary-Margaret Moore, 1986). Much to my surprise, the channeled material not only made sense, I found the content regarding emotions psychologically sound.

In one memorable communication, Bartholomew described how, in experiencing a disturbing emotion, we often construct a *mental impression* of the emotion—be it anger, resentment, sadness, or whatever—in order to *think* about it, instead of *feeling* the emotion. For example, in the midst of sadness our mind might tell us we should be smiling and cheerful. This occurs because too often, when we were young and expressed such emotions, caretakers would switch attention by saying, "Have a piece of cake and you'll feel better" or "Big boys don't cry." Many of us are never told emotions are natural, and we are not educated in ways to deal with them effectively. Instead we are conditioned *not to feel* them but to think about them. What is needed is *to feel* an emotion, to accept it, and to allow its natural movement, which then begins the process of release that furthers change and growth in a constructive way.

This last sentence encapsulates the practice that the psychologist learned in his meditations regarding the right use of emotions:

Open, Expand, Connect, and Follow (OECF). It is remarkable how these two different sources of channeled information—one being Bartholomew and the other the Gang—delivered the same content.

As I have said, this elderly psychologist evidenced a profound wisdom complemented by a copious amount of emotional and spiritual maturity. Following his recommendation, I began to contact spirit beings available to me almost on a daily basis, and I recorded the conversations on paper, word for word. The OECF practice routinely became a part of this meditation. Notably, contemporary psychology now strongly advocates the use of such meditative practices, since there is increasing scientific evidence of mental- health benefits.

My first contact in January of 2012 with such beings, whom I address as Powers That Be, resulted in the following exchange: "I ask you to be present to me as I ask for your support, protection, guidance, and insight. It seems the rage I'm experiencing is related to my inability to break through my feelings of unworthiness that stem back to the Jesus Christ event and result in terror and obsessiveness regarding my sexuality and creativity. Please comment."

> *You are very right about all of this. It is time for you to begin to dismantle this dilemma in a more concrete way. Brain Dynamics will help you a lot, along with your ability to look for cues as to what to do in your daily life. We are pleased you are contacting us in this way and are here for you.*

Confluence of Knowledge

For the sake of clarity, my reference to the "Jesus Christ event" involves a past life. I realize that some—perhaps many—readers may not believe in past lives or reincarnation. Nonetheless, this is the framework in which this experience occurred. Moreover, this communication with the Powers That Be demonstrates the harmony of several healing modalities that combined to help me change and grow.

When I was told by a channeler that I lived as a female in the time of Christ and was a friend of his, this information resonated deeply within me as truth. As a Catholic, I had had several unusual experiences in which I felt I knew Jesus personally. The channeler also told me that, when I was fourteen years of age in that lifetime, I approached Jesus regarding having a sexual relationship with him (in that era it was not unusual for fourteen-year-old females to marry or bond with a male). Jesus told me our relationship was not of that nature—that we had a platonic friendship. I was devastated by his response and left in shame and humiliation and never had contact with him again. Throughout many subsequent lifetimes, which included several in which I was a nun or a monastic person, I felt unworthy. Healthy expressions of creativity and sexuality were foreign to me. Not wanting to face the reality of my feelings, rage and obsessive behaviors became a convenient cover. In my present life, psychotherapy, journeying, and Brain Dynamics all confirmed that these remained fundamental challenges.

The Powers That Be described themselves as existing in the Upper World. In the shamanic journeys I had done up to that point, I only visited the Lower World and communed with power animals or spirit beings. I had avoided the Upper World because I sensed that the spiritual beings who dwelled there were males, and because of my sexual abuse, I shied away from unknown, powerful males. Now, with the Powers That Be, my path was leading into areas where I felt vulnerable and unsure, but their guidance helped me move forward. In fact, the phrase "journey to new health" was used in a series of meditations that followed, which I did alone and also asked the psychologist to do on my behalf, in consultation with the Gang.

The information he received affirmed me and bolstered my courage to proceed, especially concerning my process of feeling emotions of terror, rage, and sadness. I understood that I was healing across the entire history of my experience, that I was now strong enough to advance my recovery from past injuries. My ancient armor had to go. With the resources available to me from the beings and with new awareness and energy, I felt secure enough to proceed. In ensuing months I did numerous meditations, the content of which included:

- addressing my doubt about the reality of the presence of the Gangs/Powers That Be, which They assured me was absolute;
- the experience of breathing into my pelvis and how this is the seat of my power, creativity, sexuality, spirituality, and joy and how new neurological connections were being forged with this breathing technique; and
- how all this relates to *Kundalini*—the term that comes from yogic philosophy and denotes feminine *Shakti,* or bodily energy. In Eastern religious or spiritual traditions, Kundalini is described as an indwelling of spiritual energy that can be awakened to purify the body and ultimately bestow a state of divine union upon the seeker of truth. Kundalini awakened leads to deep meditation, enlightenment, and bliss and entails energy physically moving up the central channel of the spine to the top of the head-crown chakra, where one experiences wisdom, transcendence, and universality. Many systems of yoga focus on its awakening through meditation, breathing, and chanting of mantras. In physical terms, the experience is described as feeling an electric current running along the spine. (See Chapter 9 for more on Kundalini.)

Dreams also flowed into the healing energy of this time, and communications with the Powers That Be (as I referred to them) during 2012 and 2013 involved their interpretations. Especially memorable was one about a male relative that reflected my fear of death and the impact of his sexual abuse of me. It was explained that the male relative was highly sexualized and played that theme out with me, and then confirmed that I had done a grand job of healing from that abuse. They explained further that sex and death are very intertwined—the "letting go" and "giving up of the self" in sexual union are somewhat akin to death—and this male relative had an immense fear of death because of his misuse of sex.

Another dream involved the house I occupied when I lived in the country. The Powers That Be told me the dream was a reminder of a time in the 1990s when I undertook the task of self-nurturing in a house that contained my experience, provided needed safety, and wrapped me in love. I accomplished a great deal in those years, yet the internalization of a "holding environment"—a state where I felt safe, protected, and soothed—had yet to be completed, as I faced deeper realizations of the vastness of my sexual, emotional, physical, and spiritual abuse. I was told that my mother, who in some ways did love me, was unable to provide me with a loving "container" presence that was deep and strong.

About this time, a new modality helped me establish a nurturing holding environment: the practice known as Ho'oponopono. This is an ancient Hawaiian method in which a person identifies painful thoughts or emotions within the self and understands how they cause imbalance and disease. In taking responsibility for the problem, the person chooses to say: "I love you (my fear, my rage, etc.). I'm sorry. Please forgive me. Thank you." (See Chapter 10 for a more detailed account of this method.)

I applied this highly curative technique in the following way: "I love you, infant Jeannette. I'm sorry. Please forgive me. I'm sorry for neglecting you. Thank you." I felt absolutely on target as I imagined holding my infant self and nurturing her. Fortunately, I did not have to repeat this for the same countless hours I had cried alone as a child. Such healing happens in a faster way than I had imagined, due to the growth of new cells in the brain (i.e., neuroplasticity) that create healthier and more nourishing behaviors and attitudes. Again, the reader can see how the simplest of concepts often delivers the most potent results.

My healing eventually progressed to a degree where I felt able to continue writing my second book, *Grow Up Your Ego: Ten Scientifically Validated Stages to Emotional and Spiritual Maturity*, which I began in the late 1990s. I continued to write, finish, and publish that book during the early, mid, and final years of my ssecond sabbatical. The Powers That Be were 100 percent supportive and their encouragement continues through writing this book.

Communications with the Powers That Be during 2014 and 2015 included addressing the importance of nursing infant Jeannette during my daily journeying. In addition, I prayed to and connected with Our Lady of Guadalupe (see Chapter 4), which in turn contributed to the opening of pathways in my brain for the rise of Kundalini energy. No matter the difficulty or challenge, I proceeded in my healing trajectory and increasingly became able to connect my emotions to the peace, pleasure, power, purity, and passion in my pelvis. As the connection between my pelvis and heart strengthened, my heart opened with unconditional love.

One dream from that period reflected my progress. It involved my sexual attraction to a disabled male who was accompanied by an infant boy. The Powers That Be explained this was a hallmark, as I had struggled with feelings of disdain for both disabled people and infants and children. Yet in the dream, I was completely reveling and rejoicing in their presence and in my connection to them. The Powers That Be described my dreams as a night school, where I was blessed with new learning.

Soon they informed me that I was ready to slowly begin to see clients again and that I should also focus on completing my third book. Their guidance continued regarding nursing infant Jeannette, and they emphasized how this intertwined with the feeling of pleasure in my pelvis. Sexuality exists in human beings from conception to death, which most definitely applies to my experience now, including nursing infant Jeannette and self- pleasuring.

A final example of a Powers That Be communication pertained to my feelings of rage and terror, which grew particularly strong during

Holy Week, with all the connotations and trappings of Catholic dogma and tradition. They explained that Twylah, the Native American elder I studied with and who had crossed over, totally represents my shamanic heritage, which supersedes Catholicism both in my past lives and in earthly reality. Furthermore, I could rely on her constant presence and help.

My feelings of rage, though, continued to confuse me; I had wanted to believe rage was a thing of the past. However, the Powers That Be explained that as I embraced nonlinear reality in a more expanded way, surfacing of that rage fit right in with Holy Week and was necessary, because I had managed to experience it in a natural way, through a journeying experience, without harming myself or others. "Yes," They said, "there is mystery surrounding all of this, but be assured you are not crazy. Your advancement, day by day, garners more strength, presence, and commitment to completely heal yourself."

I had allowed myself to learn through numerous pathways that were, at times, strange and scary. That these paths—brain dynamics, OECF/FACE, channeling, psychotherapy, dreams—converged made my journey a healing and transformative one.

In Chapter 6, additional ways of healing, both scientific and non-scientific, will be presented. In this chapter, various ways of healing have been explained and illustrated. It is understandable that some readers may be skeptical about this information. Whether you believe or disbelieve, as the author of this book I have presented the course of events that unfolded in my life truthfully. Perhaps in the future you will encounter similar healing experiences that involve taking a "spider time out" in one way or another and be encouraged by knowing that others have traveled a comparable course and greatly benefited from it. At the same time, readers who have had such experiences can vouch for their validity and possibly choose to share with others.

WORKS CITED

Germer, C. K. (2009). *The mindful path to self-compassion: Freeing yourself from destructive thoughts and emotions.* New York: Guilford Press.

Moore, M. (1968). *Bartholomew: I come as a brother: A remembrance of illusions.* Taos, New Mexico: High Mesa Press.

Vitale, J. & Hew Len, I (2007). Zero *limits: The secret Hawaiian system for wealth, health, peace and* more. Hoboken, New Jersey: John Wiley & Son, Inc.

Chapter 4

Restoring the Feminine

HOW IS INFORMATION in the first three chapters relevant to the paradoxical return of the feminine? The answer is multifaceted. First, you learned about the history of the feminine, especially in Sumerian and Minoan cultures, and appreciated the importance of both men and women expressing their feminine energy. Second, my own story illustrates the ability of any female to convert outdated behaviors and attitudes into transformed ways of living and being. My accomplishment of such—in my seventies and complicated by PTSD—indicates you can do the same, no matter your age or circumstance, if you make the commitment to reconcile past wounds. There are numerous modalities that can help you heal. An additional factor involves grasping the importance of restoring feminine power, which is the topic of this chapter.

Men and women alike have the need and ability to restore feminine power. "Women have learned to become more like men. Now men need to learn to become more like women." This Twitter communication by Melinda Gates, co-founder (with her husband, Bill Gates) of the Gates Foundation, depicts the nature of women's pursuit of power and equality while also emphasizing the way in which men are challenged to change.

One notable way men build their feminine energy is through parenting. An illuminating, recent long-term study of Filipino men discovered that becoming a father lowers a man's testosterone level—this being correlated to how much time is spent caring for children. Contrary to one of the myths that males are biologically hardwired to violence and promiscuity, the results of this study show that men are more biologically malleable than previously thought:

> Indeed, once we [males] make the commitment to become active fathers to our children, it seems our hormones naturally shift to help sustain us in the all-important work of caregiving. As it turns out, the claim that women are "just built to be more nurturing" is baseless. The real truth is that we are hardwired to be adaptable, built to have seasons in our lives of both public ambition and domestic tenderness. Far from being an obstacle to our humanity, it turns out our best-known hormone is love's surprisingly accommodatingally (http:/.com/newsroom/hardwiredto-nurture-what–the new-testosterone-study).

In another study, 465 men in the Philippines participated in the Cebu Longitudinal Health and Nutrition Survey in 1983, when the participants were one year old. At age 21.5, researchers tested the single male participants' testosterone levels when they woke and when they went to sleep. The measurements were repeated at age 26 (in 2009), when about half of the participants had become fathers. Single men showed a small, age- related decline of about 12 to 15 percent in the male sex hormone. Testosterone levels of new fathers dropped about 30 percent. It appears men's biology responds to the physical, emotional, and psychological changes that occur with newborns. Higher testosterone has been linked with increased risk-taking and competition with other males. This might explain why lower levels occurred with greater child-care investment (http:www.livescience.com/16017-fatherhood-lowers-manly-homone -dad-home.html).

In contrast, the challenges facing women in modern times have tended to distance them from their feminine energy. Several decades ago female executives and leaders took on male characteristics and behaviors as a way to cultivate influence. Such women dressed in suits with shoulder pads, and briefcases replaced purses. Many replicated male political maneuvers and aggressive tactics. They imitated the kind of power we know men demonstrate. Few actualized the possibility of *balancing male and female equality*. Yet this remains a possibility for anyone in business—or outside of it.

At this time in history, it is fitting for all to understand that restoring feminine power does not mean curtailing male power but instead requires the promotion of balance between masculine and feminine strengths. What would this look like? Males would give up the tendency to issue orders to others and replace this with obtaining information and input. They would negotiate and gather all relevant facts. They would honor the emotional factors involved, which are often overlooked. And females would build self-confidence and be assertive, leading and teaching others.

Imagine a workplace dispute where an employee becomes very angry when he is told to work overtime, and his boss feels that he is disrespecting her authority. It may well be that the worker isn't protesting about the additional workload but rather is upset by the conflict the extra hours presents: he has an obligation to pick up children from school or day care. Similarly, the female boss needs to hone her confidence and believe in her inner strengths, her ability to plan and organize, and her intelligence, which are equal to males. If these two explored what the anger was about, an entirely different picture would emerge and hopefully allow for a fresh and more feminine approach and satisfactory resolution to the situation.

The phenomenon of male-female hierarchies is ageless; it will take time to balance out, and it will require awareness of one's inner life. As females increasingly take on leadership roles, they need to become more aware of when and how they paradoxically underestimate themselves and yet set higher standards for themselves.

That many, male and female, see a woman as "less than" yet expect her to "do it all," is embedded human culture.

The Role of Mother Mary: Perspectives of Balance and Imbalance

Consider the paradoxical example of the Catholic portrayal of the Virgin Mary, a female who is greatly revered yet not venerated as much as her son. Recent books and treatises present an alternate perspective in which Mary manifests the feminine principle on an equal par with the masculine. This is a perspective Carl Jung (1973) strongly put forth. In his discussions of archetypes—a psychological pattern or component of the mind resulting from the accumulated experience of humankind that includes expressions in all people, times, and places—he presents the archetype of Mary's feminine affiliation with Mother Earth. This is in contrast to Jesus's masculine association with the Heavenly Father. In Jung's description of how visions of Mary by people on earth increased in the twentieth century during a time of great strife, he emphasizes how her feminine influence is needed to offset male dominance. Jung presents Mary as an intercessor equivalent to her son.

In *Untie the Strong Woman: Blessed Mother's Immaculate Love for the Wild Soul*, author Clarissa Pinkola Estes (2013) describes how the Blessed Mother's inspiration reaches far beyond Catholicism. Estes maintains Mary displays herself as a living human person, who supersedes all saints. Her mission is to publicly put back into place strength and steadfastness of that which is feminine—compassion, love, and mercy. This shows up in many ways and places. From Estes's stance, all that is necessary is to ask for her help and she will be present:

> Thus, all we have to do is heart-call, and she will make her way through walls and across water, under mountains and through iron gilded bars to make

herself known. All we have to do is *remember her*, and she is instantly with us—teaching, re-centering us in her spiritual outlook, hiding us, comforting us, helping us to truly see (p. 3).

Furthermore, she can make her presence known in our thoughts, dreams, inner knowing, and unexpected perceptions. Many have experienced her presence in their lives and in various aspects. The determining factor is this: does her influence make your life better, holier?

In *Women Who Run with the Wolves* (1992), Estes describes Mary as a hell's angel, a gang leader, steering females along a wild path toward their truer selves, where they can embrace their power and explore their unconscious. She demonstrates entirely different behaviors than other saints and revered ones. Also referred to as the "Black Madonna," she is queen of the unconscious, where both positive and negative aspects of the self can reside. She looks at this earthly world and radiates light that lets us see into the dark—the source of Immaculate Love—that which remains in our unconscious and is not yet manifest. Put another way, it is love that enables us to see that the unconscious holds the "positive" as well as the "negative." When we think of bringing something to the light from the dark, we meet the Black Madonna because we are taking a chance by choosing a new, more nourishing, and more integrated way of dealing with ourselves, family, friends, and coworkers.

In an article entitled "The Return of the Black Madonna: A Sign of Our Times or How the Black Madonna Is Shaking Us Up for the Twenty-First Century," Matthew Fox notes that in Mexico she is known as "Our Lady of Guadalupe," and she holds a special place in the religious life of Mexico. It is reported she appeared to an Aztec convert to Catholicism named Juan Diego and asked that a shrine to her be built where she had appeared—now a suburb of Mexico City. Our Lady of Guadalupe's role in Mexican history involved more than religious concerns, as she has played an important part in Mexican nationalism and identity. In 1810 she was promoted as the patroness of the revolt of Miguel Hidalgo-Costilla against the Spanish. Her image appeared on banners, and the rebels' battle cry was "Long Live Our Lady of Guadalupe"—a distinct representation of the integration of masculine and feminine energies.

Fox describes her as Dark, and she summons us into the dark and thus into our depths—where divinity resides and where the true self exists. She invites us into the mystery of darkness and welcomes us to feel at home there.

When the Blessed Virgin Mary is portrayed as the Black Virgin or Black Madonna, she is said to represent our hidden past experiences, qualities, and distortions of past incarnations. When the energy of salvation reverberates in our psyches and transformation occurs, the feminine principle manifests in our conscious minds and we follow the guidance of true inner self and voice. The Black Virgin, according to esoteric tradition, represents hidden feminine qualities not yet ready to be manifested through each of us. This includes transformative powers and all the characteristics of nature and Mother Earth, which make us truly spiritual beings, whether male or female.

To respect our shadows and darkness is also to respect people of color, which is the opposite of racism. The Black Madonna invites us to honor our lower chakras, which include our relationship to the cosmos, our sexuality, and our anger and moral outrage. She will not accept flights from our depths or avoidance of the discovery of our soul's purpose, which embraces the intensities of awe, wonder, delight, creativity, and joy.

Certainly this is a far cry from how Mary has regularly been presented in the Christian world, in which her purity, virginity, and giving birth to Jesus Christ are considered either a matter of fact or faith. Of course, there is no scientific proof. Nonetheless, increasing numbers of women report the positive effects of Mary's intercession in and blessing of their lives. As males and females who strive to own our feminine power, we can learn a great deal from the way in which

Matthew Fox, Carl Jung, and Clarissa Pinkola Estes present Mary's essence and tremendous power. According to Fox:

> The Black Madonna, the goddess, provides the womb of the universe as the cosmic lap where all creatures gather. An ancient hymn underscores her cosmic role as sovereign over all of nature and the queen of all the gods and goddesses (Fox, 2011, p. 4).

In other words, the Black Madonna, the Lady of Guadalupe, is also a lover and soother of all mankind. In this regard, I feel a personal connection to Our Lady of Guadalupe/Black Madonna: When I journey to the Upper World where spirit helpers take the form of human beings, it is she and Seneca Elder Twylah Nitsch who provide me care and nurturing. To the beat of a drum, they hold me in their arms as I absorb their loving into the very cells of my entire body, brain, and being. Another major aspect of my relationship to Our Lady of Guadalupe/Black Madonna is that she helps me unearth the treasure of my unconscious mind that contributes so much transformative energy to my emotional and spiritual well-being. Such unearthing is found to occur far more in females and surely is the reason more females seek psychotherapy than males.

Facing One's Shadow Self

In the foreword to her profound book, *Women Who Run with the Wolves: Myths and Stories of the Wild Woman Archetype* (1992), Estes states:

> We are filled with a longing for the wild. There are few culturally sanctioned antidotes for this yearning. We were taught to feel shame for such a desire. But the shadow of Wild Woman still lurks

behind us. . . . No matter where we are, the shadow that trots behind us is definitely four footed (p. xvii).

Estes speaks in terms of how healthy wolves and healthy women have similar characteristics—they possess keen senses; they are playful, capable of devotion, and relational by nature; and they have great endurance and strength. In addition they are profoundly intuitive, dedicated to their offspring, connected with their mates, and adaptive to ever-changing circumstances.

Estes laments how, as the pristine wilderness of nature on this planet disappears, so does the comprehension of our inner nature. She depicts the task of reclaiming our inner psychic landscape as that of collecting bones— missing pieces and parts of us that have been buried due to their untamed nature. In traditional psychology, these pieces of ourselves are referred to as our "shadow selves"— characteristics our parents and caretakers did not approve of that consequently were repressed. In many families the expression of anger is not allowed, and in some, a lid is put on creativity and spontaneity, which shows how potentially positive energy is also confined to the shadow.

Elements of an individual's shadow are nonetheless evident in many ways. According to Jung, characters in dreams, myths, and fairytales are considered to be archetypes and represent different facets of our personalities (Anderson, 2014). For example, when an individual who was discouraged from seeking a college degree in architecture dreams about a talented person being congratulated for designing a unique building, such is an expression of his repressed desire to create.

The bottom line is that the energy of all that is put into the shadow, including our undeveloped talents and gifts, abets the dark side of human nature. Yet these energies that are perceived as negative, as well as those considered to be positive, are very natural for wolves to express. This does not mean human behavior should occur uncensored, yet it does mean we carry an obligation to dig up shadow bones and reclaim their expression in ways that do not harm ourselves or others.

I recently dug up a shadow bone, one day after a swim. As I was getting dressed in the locker room, I observed a woman putting a great amount of makeup on her face. She stood in front of the mirror and diligently applied mascara and lipstick in an excessive way. My judgmental self silently considered how this fortyish-year-old woman might be a prostitute (previously I had experienced a woman applying makeup at the gym who said outright that she was a prostitute).

However, when this woman, whom I will call Viola, struck up a conversation, I learned much about her and her son (whom I will call David) who was in a nursing home. A number of years ago he had taken an overdose of heroin and was rendered unconscious. Though Viola had been told that he would never regain use of the muscles in his body, he had slowly made progress and was now beginning to walk.

She then claimed her faith in God had helped her through all this—a faith she did not have until she herself some years ago was in jail (she was a drug user, among other things) and found being incarcerated a horrendous experience. At the end of her rope, she had said, "God, if you are real, I very much need your help and ask you to help me." Not only was she released from jail shortly thereafter, she also was befriended by people who assisted her in adjusting to life in a new way.

Now Viola prays every day and offers gratitude for how David is recovering and how he has no intention to use drugs again. She spoke of being hopeful David would be accepted at a rehabilitation center for brain- injured people, where he would receive special training and eventually be able to live a healthier life outside an institution. As we talked about prayer, I told her I would pray for David, and we each agreed to pray for one another.

As I prepared to leave, I hesitated and told Viola, "You have taught me a lesson." Her response was that we were intended to meet and have the conversation we did. Although she did not ask what lesson I had learned, I would have told her (if she had asked) of my initial judgment of her and how I more fully realized how detrimental it is to judge others—something I have struggled with for many years and which is a "bone" fragment, part of my disowned sexuality. I now hold Viola in my prayers with gratitude.

Returning to Oneself

Facing our shadow selves allows us to fully be ourselves. From a similar perspective, Estes devotes one chapter of her book to "returning to oneself" and dealing with our given natures. Children by nature are wild and enter into growth cycles in an instinctual way. Regrettably, as we physically mature, what is natural becomes eclipsed by the false, fabricated, commercially dominated world. A perceptible schism occurs between psyche and soul.

Estes relates the story of a lonely whale-man (representing the masculine, assertive part of a woman) who steals the fin of a whale-woman in order to copulate with her (representing the male and female parts merging). Estes suggests this lonely man represents the ego of the woman's psyche, with the ego and the soul vying for control of one's life force. The maturity of the ego is measured by how healthy a person's boundaries are and to what degree one is able to self-nurture. When we are young, the ego often dominates; yet for many, sometime during adulthood the yearning for the soul to lead comes into play—to return home to one's true self. Thus the lonely man is attempting to live the life of the soul but doesn't yet realize a relationship between the soul and ego must be spawned.

Ego maturity—and its importance in spirituality—is covered extensively in *Grow Up Your Ego: Ten Scientifically Validated Stages to Emotional and Spiritual Maturity* (Gagan, 2014), where I emphasize that the way in which parents bond with their offspring makes the difference as to whether a child's ego matures in a natural and healthy way or whether inadequate bonding results in the child who feels emotionally abandoned and enters adulthood challenged by the need to do the psychological and spiritual work to achieve ego maturity.

In *Wild Women*, Estes describes the woman who has successfully returned to self as one who:

- possesses great creativity;
- is able to self-reflect and meditate;
- knows how to nurture herself;
- is involved in altruistic endeavors;
- is appropriately assertive;
- is at peace with herself and others;
- accepts reality as it is; and
- takes pleasure in intimate relationships.

These descriptions of the wild woman archetype are very similar to the scientifically validated characteristics of the mature ego as put forth in *Grow Up Your Ego*, which include:

1. being at peace with one's inner conflicts;
2. feeling comfortable alone or with others;
3. experiencing a deepening sense of inner connectedness;
4. living in a constant flux of experiences and changing states of consciousness;
5. being aware of the illusion of a permanent individual self;
6. relying on intellect and intuition without overvaluing them;
7. being at one with the self and others as ongoing participants in creation;
8. appreciating peak and transcendent experiences that increasingly occur in the foreground;
9. welcoming a "To Be" state of awareness; and
10. participating in non-evaluative, integrative witnessing of experience and the meaning of existence.

As challenging as it may sound, returning home to one's own unique and soulful cycle is eventually realized by many. Being spiritual includes embracing the mystery of life that goes beyond finite understanding. There are many rungs on the ladder to attain this. The dilemma is we think there is something to *find* when the answer rests *within* each of us. Paradoxically, when we reach the place of not striving to be what we think we should be and feel we are what we are in the moment, the struggle to become spiritual ends and we are who we are every day. We remember that all is divine, and we begin to live in the moment. When we realize we cannot force the brain, cannot discipline our bodies, and that we have done all we can, tried as hard as we know how, and that this is not about winning, the ego gives up seeking and surrenders. The result is we realize we are enough just as we are—very akin to the paradoxical way of experiencing our emotions and allowing them to be what they are.

One of my shamanic journeys typifies this return to self and literally reflects Estes's concept of shadow bones. In my journey, a power animal rearranged my bare bones, followed by the angels channeling the glow of pumpkin-colored light into the new arrangement, solidifying it in place.

Evita

A good example of the split between ego and soul can be seen in the life of Evita, the wife of the Argentinian president Juan Peron. Curiously, in her autobiography she referred to two parts of herself, the first being Eva: an illegitimate child who in adulthood became the wife of the president and was involved in ceremonial tasks and gala functions. The second part was Evita: ". . . the wife of the Leader of the people who had entrusted to him all of its faith, all of its hope, and all its love" (Hall, 2004, p. 220). She was an icon, a real human being who identified with the poor and disadvantaged. Indeed it was her magnetism, along with her renowned inclination to work countless hours each day on their behalf, that drew people to her. Not surprisingly, Evita also demonstrated the influence of Mary the mother of God. She made good use of Marian-type symbols, gestures, and performances that resonated with the Argentine people and contributed to Evita's power and personal charisma (Hall, 2004).

Paradoxically, Evita was an adoring and somewhat subservient wife, while at the same time her status was tremendously respected and revered by common folk. Evita was given the official title of "Spiritual Leader of the Nation" by the Argentine Congress. She was a leader of her people, but authors Nicholas Fraser and Marysa Navarro, who are credited with the most- researched and factual accounting of Evita's life in their book *Evita: The Real Life of Eva Peron* (1996), point out the contradictions. Their writings make it clear how Evita was not a mirror image of Mary, since at times she demonstrated behaviors and feelings such as resentment and a strong desire to avoid humiliation—all of which stemmed from her illegitimacy and impoverished childhood. In her adulthood during a press interview, she lied in stating, "that she spoke French, that she liked to ride horses and sail, that she had been to acting school, and that she was a reader of classics and contemporaries" (p. 46).

> In 1947 when she undertook her self-styled "Rainbow Tour" of Europe, she was greeted jubilantly in Spain, and in Italy she had an audience with the Pope. Originally it was planned she would have tea with the Queen of England, but due to ill health, Evita arrived in England two weeks late and the tea party never happened. Because the Queen was unable to see Evita when she wished to see her, it was thought that she did not wish to see Evita at all. . . . In reality it had to do with feelings of wounded vanity (pp. 95-97).

The sum of this is that Evita opened the door to female-male equality while also demonstrating a female leadership role that impacted Argentina as well as other countries. At the same time, she had not honed the ability to balance her power with compassion for those who criticized her or found her unacceptable. Although some of her supporters believed she was a saint and should be canonized, this was never seriously considered by the Vatican. Evita did not feel at peace with herself and did not demonstrate an empathic attitude toward her dissenters.

Awareness of My Feminine Power

As far back as I can remember, I felt comfortable being a female. I enjoyed wearing dresses, having afternoon "tea parties" with neighborhood girlfriends, as well as discovering self-pleasuring in bed at night. Theoretically, between the ages of three and five the sexual organs become an object of interest and manipulation for children, often resulting in orgasmic masturbation. Sexual exploration and play in children are a normal part of growing up. However when one of my older sisters found out what I was doing, she admonished me and said such activity was a sin—and that put an end to it. I doubt I was old enough to even understand what a sin was.

The first time I was aware of a woman being pregnant occurred when an aunt visited and I saw how fat she had become. When I questioned an older female in my family about this, I was told that a baby was growing inside of her belly. Puzzled, I figured the only way the baby could get out of the belly was through the belly button. As with many of my generation, next to no information was given about how babies get into a mother's "belly" in the first place.

However, a neighbor girl about three years older than I spontaneously volunteered one day that she knew how that occurred. She then wrote some words on a piece of paper for me to read—the gist of which I eventually figured out to involve some part of a male being inserted into a female's body, and that the baby that resulted was then born through an opening in the female's lower parts. Indeed this was a time of the "dark ages" regarding educating children about the facts of life, which unfortunately casts a shadow on sexuality and the inherent beauty of it when it is properly nurtured and expressed. Fortunately, individuals can and should fight for enlightenment and freedom to experience their sexuality. Even those like me, who have been sexually abused, can reclaim the power and pleasures of the body.

In many ways, I did look up to my three older sisters as I observed how they functioned as females. Two of them married shortly after graduating from high school and had happy marriages, with each giving birth to several children. The eldest, however, entered a three-year training program for nurses. As you've read, she later urged me to attend a university that offered a bachelor's degree in nursing. At that time most nursing school programs were for three years, with degrees in nursing relatively few. At one point there was a "capping" ceremony, when students were given a white cap to wear—no longer a tradition—that was an insignia of professional standing. And of course, passing a state exam was necessary to practice as a professional nurse. Even though the program I attended had no males, I found nurses and nursing students were highly valued by physicians and other staff. I felt proud to be a nurse.

When I married and had children, my role as a wife and mother became paramount. I wanted to have children, and surely my feminine power was experienced as I welcomed the pregnancy and birth of each of my five children. As they grew up and became increasingly independent, my perspective changed. I sought to experience and express my feminine power in a new way. Though I wouldn't have described it as such then, I sought a way of daily living that welcomed and blended feminine and masculine energies. I very much wanted a career that would allow me to convey the totality of who I was and who I was becoming—a mental health professional, a psychologist, an author, a shamanic healer, and a leader in my fields of expertise—each of which entails feminine and masculine energy and power. The feminine is evidenced in my ability to listen to clients and to intuitively respond with insights, compassion, and guidance. The masculine manifests when I more publicly teach and lead others into levels of emotional and spiritual understanding and growth. In the mid- and late-1990s, after publishing the *Journeying* book, I gave seminars and presentations both in New Mexico and in other states. My ability to teach and lead others had reached a pinnacle, yet as you've read, confronting emotional obstacles to growth and healing "shadow" aspects of myself was an ongoing necessity.

WORKS CITED

Anderson, H. (2014). *Maleficent: What do fairy tales really mean?* Retrieved from http://.bbc.com/culture/story/201440602-secret-meanings-of-fairy-tales

Estes, C. P. (1992). *Women who run with the wolves: Myths and stories of the wild woman archetype.* New York: Ballantine Books.

Estes, C. P. (2013). *Untie the strong woman: Blessed mother's immaculate love for the wild soul.* Louisville, CO: Sounds True.

Fox, M. (February 21, 2011). *The return of the black Madonna; A sign of our times or how the black Madonna is shaking us up for the twenty-first century.* Retrieved from http://.interfaithssevicesofthelowcountry.com/insightsinto-the- black-madonna-by-matthew-fox

Fraser, N. & Navarro, M. (1996). *Evita: The real life of Eva Peron.* New York: W.W. Norton & Company.

Gagan, J. M. (1998). *Journeying: Where shamanism and psychology meet.* Santa Fe, NM: Rio Chama Publications.

Gagan, J. M. (2014). *Grow up your ego: Ten scientifically validated stages to emotional and spiritual maturity.* Santa Fe, NM: Rio Chama Publications.

Gates, M. (November 16, 2015). Twitter communication.

Hall, L. B. (2004). *Mary, mother and warrior: The virgin in Spain and the Americas.* Austin, TX: University of Texas Press.

Jung, C. J. (1973). *Answer to Job.* Princeton, NJ: Princeton University Press.

Males who nurture information retrieved from http://.com/newsroom/hardwiredto-nurture-what–the new-testosterone-study and http://www.livescience.com/16017-fatherhood-lowers-manly-homone-dad-home.html

Chapter 5

Characteristics of a Goddess

FROM THE FALL of the feminine to the restoring the feminine in our lives, from Mother Mary to the Black Madonna, we have been discussing the concept of the goddess—the ideal of embodied feminine energy. We started with a holistic perspective, and now we will look closely at the parts of this whole by returning to the attributes presented by Sheryl Sandburg (Chapter 1). Women can be effective leaders and manifest a goddess-like nature by cultivating:

1. Self-confidence
2. The ability to negotiate with the myth of having to do it all
3. The courage to seek and speak one's truth
4. Relationships with a true partner

Confidence

Sandberg presents data from numerous studies that show females underestimate themselves, which reflects a lack of self-confidence. Likewise, females rate their work performance as worse than it actually is, while males rate their performance as better than it actually is. The genesis of this disparity rests with gender-based expectations.

From birth, boys are treated differently than girls. Research indicates parents talk to girl babies more than to boy babies, resulting in boys not being as communicative, especially regarding emotions. Mothers often overestimate crawling ability in boys and underestimate it in girls, causing boys to be more athletic and physical. By believing girls need more help than boys, mothers frequently spend more time comforting and hugging infant girls, which results in girls being more comfortable with touching and comforting others. In contrast, mothers are more likely to allow their infant boys to play by themselves, which leads to boys to being more independent (Sandberg, 2014) and, thus, more confident.

Furthermore, cultural assessments—such as girls are pretty and boys are smart—broaden into the idea that boys are leaders while girls who lead are "bossy." Stereotypically, boys are said to be better at math and science than girls. Readers of this book no doubt have their own stories of how differences between girls and boys played out in their childhood, teenage years, and on into adulthood.

Doing It All

The myth of having to do it all is also an extension of this early conditioning. Here we enter the territory of comparison: (a) comparison to colleagues who may be men and most likely have fewer responsibilities at home; and (b) comparison to mothers who stay home to take care of their children. Consider the story of the woman who was a mother of two children. She was a bookkeeper in a large organization and routinely took work home. After spending time with her children in the evening, she stayed up late into the night, completing work tasks. She described her life as exhausting, plus she was riddled with guilt because she believed stay-at-home mothers were better mothers and believed her coworkers, who seemed to manage their workload during work hours, were better employees.

Though common, these perspectives are not supported by the research. A study done in 1991 by the Early Child Research Network found that: "Children who were cared for exclusively by their mothers did not develop differently than those who were also cared for by others." This woman's comparison to coworkers is another matter, and it is probable she similarly is burdened by other false assumptions. Are her standards too high? Are her coworkers as meticulous as she is about assignments? If she is evaluated by her supervisor as a valued employee, does she allow herself to accept that as true? If she is assessed as lacking in some area of job performance, does she realize how many other workers are noted for their flaws—that no one is perfect?

Speaking Truth

Seeking and speaking one's truth is usually easier for women than for men, at least in the personal arena. Because speaking the truth involves emotions, women are better adjusted to this terrain, in part because they typically have a larger limbic system than males, which makes them more in touch with and expressive of their emotions. Studies also show that mothers teach girls more about emotions than they teach boys.

However, women expressing their truth and emotions in the workplace (or other public environments) is another matter, especially for those in lower positions. Many individuals have not developed the skills for communicating their feelings without making others feel defensive. Speaking the truth is more effective when we realize that what is true for me may not be true for you. Learning to convey one's perspective is typically helped by using an "I" statement versus "You." For example, "You never finish things on schedule" is likely to be received as an accusation. Rephrased, it can more easily be heard and accepted: "I feel frustrated when you don't meet deadlines and welcome suggestions you have for correcting that" (see Chapter 8 of this book for more examples).

Effective communication is, of course, necessary for true leaders (as opposed to dictators). Sandberg references Marcus Buckingham and others who are challenging beliefs about leadership. "Their research suggests that presenting leadership as a list of carefully defined qualities (like strategic, analytical, and performance-oriented) no longer holds. Instead, true leadership stems from individuality that is honestly and sometimes imperfectly expressed" (Sandberg, 2014, p. 91).

Partnership

Attitudes and approaches that create a good marriage can be applied to any relationship. Making your partner a true partner involves connecting with another person in as positive a way as possible. Whether in a marriage relationship or with a friend, coworker, supervisor, or even with living goddesses—those who embody confidence, balance, and the ability to live and speak their truth make good partners. These qualities can be nurtured by both males and females, and when mastered, they strengthen the individual as well as the partnership. Chapter 8 will delve deeply into understanding this ideal, and the feminine in relationships will be explored more closely.

Living Goddesses

I encourage all readers to manifest the goddess in themselves. Feminine energy is not "out there"; it is innate within each of us. If dormant, it can be awakened; if present and alive, it can be strengthened. I conclude this chapter by sharing three examples of living goddesses: Jane Little and my friends Becky and Zelda.

My Friend Becky

I met Becky when I was twelve years old. We each were entering junior high—she from a country grade school and me from the town grade school. We quickly connected on several levels as good students with musical talents and a curiosity about life beyond the small community we lived in. Throughout high school we spent hours talking about how we wanted to move to a city and experience life in a much broader way. Since I obtained a driver's license before she did, I would drive us around in a "Banana Truck" which was a delivery truck owned by my older brother who had a produce business. Laughter was a given as we explored many places and spoke candidly of our hopes and desires for a great future.

When we graduated from high school, she went to Stephens College and I attended Marquette University in Wisconsin. Upon completion she returned briefly to our hometown to teach public school music in several nearby mining towns. Although born to be a teacher with an innate love for children, the urge to satisfy another interest drove her to Mills College in California for a degree in interior design. For a number of years she practiced design professionally in San Francisco. She was introduced to a nationally published and recognized designer with whom she worked on projects across the country. I once enjoyed staying in the hotel that she had been commissioned to decorate in New Orleans.

The next thing I knew she had been swept off her feet by a rich man from a foreign country whom she married. Unbeknownst to Becky and to her great shock, when they arrived in the foreign country where he lived she discovered he had had two wives who were deceased and sixteen living children. After this brief interlude in 1976 she was ready for a new and different chapter, and returned to California to study court reporting and became a top-notch legal secretary and traveled the U.S. with litigation teams of a prominent law firm. On yearly vacations she traveled often to exotic places, which helped satisfy her desire to experience the world in a more expansive way.

Throughout all these years we communicated via telephone and email as well as sometimes visiting each other. Becky engaged in psychotherapy at various times throughout these years, which helped decrease the emotional confusion and stress from the many changes in her life.

During a visit she made to New Mexico we, along with my two daughters, went to White Sands where there are miles of sand dunes to roll in—which we deliciously did, laughing all the way. On that same trip we went to Alamogordo to have our "auras read" by a person who was well known for doing so. We both shared a penchant for exploring the unknown as well as our spirituality. When she visited the Holy Land in 1975-1976, she said she could "see all the way to heaven," but she could never fully engage in a specific religion. Questions that came up included: "Why all the religious wars?" "What is the meaning of all this hostility?" "What and where is the 'something else'?"

In 2009 she fell and broke one of her hips in three places, and in 2013 she broke the other hip in two places, all of which involved several surgeries and an extended time of recovery. It was during this time she put spirituality on the front burner. On one occasion she heard Desmond Tutu's address that touched her heart. More recently she has become involved in the Global Higher Consciousness Movement, which is an international, multidisciplinary collaboration of scientists and engineers. Results of their studies suggest an emerging unifying field of consciousness that is described by sages in all cultures. This movement promotes the message of peace and harmony for humanity and for Earth. They sponsor gatherings during which people pray or meditate for the well-being of humankind.

In June 2015 she visited Albuquerque, New Mexico, to check out retirement communities. It was a delight to see her—here she was, using a walker but not missing a step with her wonderful sense of humor. We talked of many things, including how she was unable to dance, due to her balance and hip issues, or play the marimba or piano because of her neuropathy, but she still had her wrists and could teach drumming to sick and disadvantaged children! It was my hope she would relocate to Albuquerque, yet a recent message informed me that she now has a nice man in her life with whom she connects spiritually.

The sum of this is that at age eighty (with numerous ups and downs in her life, including recovering from thyroid cancer at age thirty), she has not only engaged in psychotherapy to resolve emotional dilemmas and acquaint herself with her shadow side, she has embraced her spirituality, expanded her consciousness, and now enjoys true partnership with a male lover. Indeed, my friend's light-heartedness, candor, and deep spirituality personify a goddess who never ages.

Jane Little

We find examples of goddesses in the news all the time. In May 2016 I was pleased to read about Jane Little. She was a member of the Atlanta Symphony Orchestra since the group's founding during World War II, who died at the age of eighty-seven after collapsing on stage. A bassist recognized by Guinness World Records for the longest professional tenure with a single orchestra, she had joined the Atlanta Youth Symphony Orchestra at age sixteen, after only two years of studying bass in high school. Years later, when she broke her pelvis and was told by the doctor she would be out for three to four months, she returned to the orchestra in two weeks!

Little's success in a role traditionally reserved for men served as an inspiration, said the orchestra's executive director, Jennifer Bariament. Described as a person with passion, vitality, spirit, and incredible talent, she did what she loved until the end of her life—a true goddess.

Zelda

My first impression of Zelda was of her terrific swimming ability—at the age of eighty her form was perfect. Later I learned she began training for swimming meets when she was eleven years old. With the mentoring of a fantastic coach and kinship with talented teammates, she trained and traveled with girls to championship meets throughout the U.S. and Canada. In her words: "The joy for me was the camaraderie of working for shared goals." This is surely an example of an ant-community time in her life and the result of her confident, "I can-do-this attitude."

Of her childhood, she emphasizes how living on a farm fostered feelings of closeness to the earth, plants, and animals. She describes this as very nourishing—absorbing daily wonderment and experiential teachings. She also knew of migrant children working alongside their parents, not having the benefits she enjoyed, such as attending good schools, being warmly dressed, and having enough to eat; this engendered a sense of compassion and gratitude early in her life. Furthermore, her mother fostered a sense of responsibility, as she had Zelda deliver fresh food and water to the migrants.

During Zelda's early years, her mother was a mentor in her life, teaching Zelda how to tend a garden and care for animals. Zelda describes her mother as a highly educated and talented woman, who had a degree from UCLA in music theory. She composed her own music for the violin and piano and played the violin with the Pasadena Symphony. She was an excellent horsewoman, devoted to her family and her husband, who adored her. She also demonstrated moral conviction and took action against the violation of civil rights, fiercely protecting a Japanese-American college student from being removed to an internment camp.

In Zelda's teen years, though, her mother didn't want Zelda to "out-do" her brother, who was a late bloomer. Worse, her mother opposed her competitive swimming career, writing down every penny spent on swimming and offering no encouragement or praise for her efforts or academic honors. When Zelda left for college she felt she was a failure—that her accomplishments meant nothing. The devaluation she felt would persist through many stages of her life, presenting numerous challenges and opportunities for change and growth.

In particular and in part because her mother approved, Zelda married a man, which resulted in a troubled marriage. When she became pregnant with her fifth child, the doctor offered termination of the pregnancy, to which she agreed. When she woke in the recovery room, she was crying. The woman in the next bed, a psychology student, said to the nurse, "She needs to cry"— providing Zelda with an excellent example of the feminine expression and support of emotions.

Zelda refers to this time in her life as living a double life: the one before the world, where they were upstanding family, and the one behind the scenes, where the troubled marriage relationship continued. Eventually she summoned the courage to share the truth of her life with a psychotherapist. In the end, Zelda initiated a separation from her husband, with the matter of pleasing her mother no longer an issue. A long course of therapy helped Zelda move beyond the difficulty of her marriage into acceptance and forgiveness—for herself and for her ex-husband.

Career-wise, she began to blossom. Zelda engaged in a number of activities, including being a teacher and a volunteer in organizations aimed at improving and balancing society. Later she was the executive director of the American Diabetes Association of metropolitan northern New Jersey and New York. Even though being in charge of such a large organization was demanding, she loved the challenges of a variety of public education programs and fundraising events.

Zelda became an environmentalist and later an outspoken feminist. All these activities confirm that, as her life unfolded, she increasingly tapped into her power, spoke her truth, and displayed a blend of female and male energy. Moreover, she shared her talents as a mentor to many others.

Enduring numerous disappointments and losses in her life— including the tragedies of her mother's suicide and a daughter's struggle with disease and premature death—Zelda has learned a great deal and chooses to live in as positive way as she can. She says that the trajectory of her life has evolved into greater expressiveness in her music.

When she moved to Santa Fe, she served on the board of the Santa Fe Symphony. She has a grand piano in her living room, which she plays often, and music provides constant stimulus for her creative energies.

Other daily activities include enjoying her home and sharing it with visitors. She has many art objects that she offers for sale—money being a factor, since she relies on limited retirement funds.

Recently Zelda fell and broke her upper femur, which is on the mend. However a medical condition involving her heart and lungs requires her to be on oxygen twenty-four hours a day, which curtails her activities. What is outstanding about Zelda's life is that early on she did not hesitate to express herself in creative, leadership, and feminine ways.

Peace Ambassadors

Surely a common thread among goddesses is that of being peace ambassadors. Through dedication to their purpose in life—whether realized in early adulthood, middle, or later years, they creatively weave peaceful energies into their pursuits and relationships. As such they reflect the goals of the Global Prosperity and Peace Initiative—an organization launched at an international event in November 2016 at Salt Lake City, Utah, USA.

This organization, which involves both male and female members, is being implemented in 196 nations with the goal "to increase the level of love, prosperity, and peace in the world." It behooves each and every one of us to take note of this initiative, as it involves approaching problems world-wide in a peaceful way. More information can be found at http://.ProsperityandPeaceInitiative.org.

WORKS CITED

Buckingham. M. (2012). Leadership development in the age of the algorithm. *Harvard Business Review* 90, no. 6 (pp. 86-94); and George, B. et al. (2007). Discovering your authentic leadership. *Harvard Business Review* 85, no. 2 (pp. 129-138).

Gagan, J. M. (2014). *Grow up your ego: Ten scientifically validated stages to emotional and spiritual maturity.* Santa Fe, NM: Rio Chama Publications.

Jung, C. J. (1967). *Symbols of transformation* (2nd ed.) in *The collected works*, vol. 5., Bollingen Series, XX, trans. R.F.C. Hull. Princeton, NJ: Princeton University Press.

Sandberg, S. (2014). *Lean in: Women, work and the will to lead.* New York: Alfred A. Knopf.

Weil, A. (1995). Spontaneous healing. New York: Knopf.

Chapter 6

Ways To Welcome One's Goddess

IN THE FOREGOING stories, Becky, Jane, and Zelda exemplify women who have welcomed their goddess. Intriguingly, males as well as females can develop the goddess in themselves. Women welcoming their inner goddess involves tapping into male qualities of power—previously buried confidence, logic, assertiveness, and risk taking—and learning how to bring those qualities to life in the most constructive ways. Men welcoming their inner goddess entails embracing characteristics of empathy, self-control, collaboration, learning from mistakes, and cultivating nurturing and equality.

There are as many ways to accomplish this as there are individuals who seek to do so. Some readers may already be experiencing the characteristics of a more mature ego, which includes the spiritual qualities of a goddess. Others will realize there are steps and stages toward reaching such a pinnacle. Following are scientific and non-scientific paths to bring out the goddess in you.

Therapy

If a person seeks professional help, finding a trusted psychotherapist with whom there is a strong rapport is pivotal. Listings on the Internet of therapists who are licensed social workers, psychologists, or counselors may be a good start. Consulting with others who have pursued this route may or may not result in a recommendation that is a good fit. Many therapists will provide an initial consultation (usually less than an hour) during which questions can be asked, with the resulting dialogue helping one decide if this therapist is appropriate. Even if so, after several sessions the individual may decide the therapist isn't a good match. Sometimes in sharing this with the therapist, the therapist can suggest several names of others who might be a correct choice.

Psychotherapy healing modalities also include group therapy and/or being a part of a group devoted to increasing a woman's femininity and power. In both instances, it is important the group focus on the positives of feminine pursuits while not indulging in male bashing. The bottom line is that equality between the feminine and masculine exist with sufficient balance of power. Masculinity emphasizes ambition, assertiveness, being tough, and focusing on material success. Femininity highlights caring and nurturing behaviors, environmental awareness, and concern with the quality of life.

Self-help

Another way of welcoming one's goddess is through reading relevant information. There are countless numbers of books listed on the Internet. As previously mentioned, *Grow Up Your Ego: Ten Scientifically Validated Stages to Emotional and Spiritual Maturity* details the ten stages of growth and provides questions and exercises that aid readers to identify their present stage of growth and steps to advance to the next stage. A major reason I wrote this book was to assure growth seekers that science has demonstrated that the ego *can* and *will* mature, given the right environment.

If you were to ask which chapter of the book is most useful and consequential, I would immediately answer the fifth chapter, which addresses the topic of self-soothing, since the pace of ego growth greatly depends on one's ability to do so. Ideally initiated at birth, this ability to self-soothe is internalized as an infant receives consistent, loving attention. The child is then able to call on this capacity when caretakers aren't available. This ability to self-nurture calms distress and helps one surmount the obstacles and challenges of emotional growth. Here is an excerpt from *Grow Up Your Ego*:

> Research results of Harvard researcher George Vaillant (1993) solidly demonstrate that the ego matures through the *internalization of a holding environment*—that is, by holding inside ourselves the image and emotional experience of people we love and who love us. Just as infants who are fortunate enough to securely bond with their parents take in the soothing mother, we adults can connect with a nurturing source and internally anchor it to become self-soothers. The experience of being loved, valued, and treasured for who we are then lives within us, filling the aching gaps of isolation and loneliness. In other words, Vaillant is saying it is never too late for attachment!
>
> Barring neuronal damage in the developing fetus or injury to brain tissue after birth, to whatever degree we suffered inadequate bonding, opportunity to round out this experience can bring completion *no matter our age*. The internalization of a holding environment involves the phenomenon of neuroplasticity as new neurons result from a relationship with someone who takes on a parental, teaching, or emotionally nourishing role.
>
> This is why foster parenting and adoption succeed when children are received into loving, psychologically ripe environments. This is why, when we have the good fortune to find mentors

who take us under their wings, we internalize an experience worth the time and energy of someone who treasures us and who may help us resurrect parts of ourselves our parents ignored or even tried to eradicate. This is why relationships steeped in tolerance, patience, and commitment touch hidden pockets of potential we ultimately dare to manifest. This is why it is argued that when God and spiritual deities are taken in as attachment figures, that connection with sources emanating unconditional love opens our hearts (Gagan, 2014).

Neuroplasticity again makes it understandable that growth is possible at any age. The brain's role in spirituality continues to be studied, and it is not surprising that we find differences between male and female brains. Daniel Amen, a psychiatrist, neuroscientist, and brain-imaging expert, includes spirituality as a component of brain function. In his book *Unleash the Power of the Female Brain* (2013), he details the anatomical and physiological features of both female and male brains. The use of SPECT (single-photon emission computed tomography) scans of the brain over a twenty-two-year period have resulted in a database of 78,000 scans. This data shows areas of the brain that work well and display good activity in addition to areas that are either low or high in activity. Studies comparing 26,000 healthy, age-matched male and female SPECT scans showed women had significantly increased brain activity compared to men in seventy of the eighty areas. Male and females are equally intelligent, but each tends to use different parts of the brain to problem solve or reach goals. Females have a higher percentage of gray matter, while males have a higher percentage of white matter. This means men use only a few key brain areas to solve problems while women draw on many areas at the same time. Females also tap into the right side of the brain more—an area considered to be the seat of the emotional and spiritual realms—as well as having larger areas in the brain that contribute to relying on and trusting their gut feelings. The outcome of this is that women tend to be far more intuitive than men. Women know when something is wrong. They are able to shift their attention, be more flexible, and go with the flow.

Dr. Amen uses the results of this research to emphasize how females benefit from learning the strengths of their brains and consistently applying them. Included among those strengths are intuition, empathy, self-control, collaboration, learning from mistakes, the ability to plan and organize, plus an appropriate amount of worry. His conclusion is that females are wired for leadership! Amen states, "Leaders everywhere are realizing that the hope of the world lies in giving opportunity to women" (p. 337). This harkens back to the very beginning of this book when I discussed the disparities between males and females and the tremendous need for females to "catch up" and bring balance to the lives of adults and children.

ASCs

There are other ways to attain a holding environment and self-soothe to welcome the goddess within. Altered states of consciousness (ASC)— sometimes referred to as *non-ordinary states*—occur when a person loses normal sense perceptions. Examples include dreaming at night, being intoxicated or strung out on drugs, and being hypnotized. ASCs can be helpful or harmful. Political leaders have been known to sway masses through their charismatic use of words and hypnotic suggestions. On the other hand, proper use of ASC can activate tremendous healing potential. Meditation, progressive relaxation, yoga, and guided imagery counteract the effects of stress and provide a quieting of the nervous system. Andrew Weil (1995), the sage of alternative medicine, states that imagery is most beneficial when it is emotion laden. An example of this might be a patient delightfully imaging an intestinal tumor being attacked by a potion that dissolves it.

A very effective ASC technique is that of Eye Movement Desensitization and Reprocessing (EMDR) that is individually tailored to a client's needs. This involves the therapist asking the client to imagine a place that feels safe and calm. The therapist then moves her fingers back and forth in front of the client's eyes until the positive emotions are consistently present. This is followed by the client being instructed to bring an image of a distressing event to mind while feeling the emotions associated with the safe image. Again she uses her eyes to track the therapist's back-and-forth finger movement. This activates brain processes that facilitate healing of a psychological dynamic frozen in time and empowers the client with the ability to self-soothe. Furthermore this involves neuroplasticity—the creation of new brain cells. To locate an EMDR practitioner near you, visit http://www.emdr.com and click "find a clinician."

Another example of connecting with an unconditionally loving figure is that of a person being with a teacher, mentor, or spiritual being while in an ASC. This can happen naturally when a person is in nature. Many life experiences involve being in a natural setting, such as in a forest, sitting next to a body of water, gazing at the moon and stars at night, or gardening in the backyard. In the quiet of such a relaxed state we may feel a connection with Mother Nature during which "light bulb" solutions to problems occur.

An acquaintance of mine frequently walks through the woods, and as she sits quietly on a bench, she drops into a soothing, meditative state. She describes these times as experiences she could not do without, as it feeds her soul. This is very related to shamanism—the oldest healing tradition known to humankind.

Shamanism

Our psychological and spiritual roots go back to cultures steeped in shamanic tradition, where the healing role fell to the tribal shaman. Use of an altered state of consciousness was routine, during which the shaman traveled to other realms to obtain healing information.

In shamanic terms, this is referred to as *journeying* and is a technique that can be learned by anyone. Several organizations teach journeying to thousands of individuals around the world in weekend trainings (www.shamanism.org and www.sandraingerman.com). Journeying allows any of us to move into an altered state of consciousness to tap inner resources and apply healing knowledge to ourselves. Carl Jung (1967) dipped into shamanic territory when he described how nature provides countless mothering archetypes that nourish and soothe us, including animals, real or not.

Self-empowering in this way, journeying resonates with the notion of individual responsibility as well as personal participation in the healing process. It provides an excellent way to connect with an unconditionally loving figure and again involves neuroplasticity—the creation of new brain cells. Furthermore, it is a healing modality for emotional disturbances such as anxiety, anger, confusion, depression, and fatigue. For many individuals, especially those dealing with trauma, healing occurs in stages. As in my case, healing one aspect of neglect and abuse resulted in an additional awareness; for example, beneath sadness and depression there was rage.

Connecting with nature, encountering helpful figures (whether imagined or real), and experiencing calm and soothing acceptance are all available to anyone who carries both healing intent and staying power for the ongoing venture. Some of us do this naturally and spontaneously. Some of us need the direction of a person trained in ASC. Once learned, ASC can be a helpful tool for the rest of our lives.

By now, it is apparent that the most difficult task I encountered in healing myself was acquiring the ability to love and nurture myself. Even though it took a considerable length of time to perfect this capacity, it was through the use of ASCs that this eventually occurred—notably through meditation and journeying and spider-like experiences of self-examination and the healing of spiritual and emotional wounds. And once again I remind you that if, in my late seventies, I was able to do this, so can you!

Non-scientific Trees of Knowledge

Trees are referred to in many ways, from being the source of good and evil to being a nurturing expression of Mother Nature. Having looked at scientific branches of knowledge like psychotherapy and ASCs, this section looks at the fruits of non-scientific modalities, including numerology, astrology, I Ching, runes, and tarot.

Numerology

We begin with numerology, which is based on the belief there is an order in the universe—from the atom to the solar system. Pythagoras, who was a philosopher, mystic, and the forefather of numerology, believed the human soul is immortal. As one of the first to introduce the idea of one God, he asserted that the purpose of human life is to let the divine into your heart.

Pythagoras further discerned what today is studied in quantum physics: that everything—when broken down into basic elements—is nothing but energy. At this subatomic level there is no matter, only energy and vibration. Everything vibrates at a different frequency. Pythagoras claimed that everything in the world—living and nonliving—followed the laws of vibration, which can be described in numbers. His theories became the foundation of present-day numerology, wherein each number has a meaning and its own vibration, just like notes in music. These conceptual qualities can help us find meaning in the mission of a human soul, in describing our personal characteristics, and in understanding how some people have it easy in life while others struggle.

We are born with a set of characteristics, and understanding these traits can help us discover and reach our full potential by recognizing the strong areas we can accentuate as well as the weak points in need of attention. In numerology human qualities are expressed in numbers 1 through 9 (zero is not used). At birth we are given four personal numbers, which describe the lessons to be learned during our lives and the spiritual growth that can be attained. The four personal numbers involve the vibrations of specific energies:

- the *Life Lesson Number*, derived from the birth date
- the *Soul Number*, derived from all the vowels in a name given at birth
- the *Outer Personality Number*, derived from all the consonants in the name
- the *Path of Destiny Number*, derived from the sum of vowels and consonants in the name

Furthermore, each letter in the alphabet is assigned a number value, with that number having a vibration of specific energy—*A* is 1, *B* is 2, *C* is three, and so forth; *Z* is 26. Letters beyond the letter *I* (which is assigned number 9) are reduced to a single digit—for example the number 12 adds up to the number 3 (1 + 2 = 3).

Let's use John Matthew Doe as a name example, with a birth date of January 1, 1955.

- The **Life Lesson Number** is 22 (1 + 1 + 1 + 9 + 5 + 5 = 22)
- The **Soul Number** is 5 ($O = 6$; $A = 1$; $A = 1$; $E = 5$; $O = 6$; $E = 5$. The total is 23, which reduces to 5).
- The **Outer Personality Number** is 3 ($J = 1$; $H = 8$; $N = 5$; $M = 4$; $T = 2$;
- $T = 2$; $H = 8$; $D = 4$. The total is 39, which reduces to 3).
- The **Path of Destiny Number** is 8 ($J = 1$; $O = 6$; $H = 8$; $N = 5$; $M = 4$; $A = 1$; $T = 2$; $T = 2$; $H = 8$; $E = 5$; $W = 5$; $D = 4$; $O = 6$; $E = 5$. The total is 62, which reduces to 8).

According to numerology, numbers 11, 22, and 33 are *master numbers* that carry greater spiritual influence, and these numbers are not reduced. The specific vibration of John's Life Lesson number, 22, indicates he is a builder who has deep spiritual understanding and facilitates use of knowledge in a practical way. This means he needs to express his inherent potential to build and accomplish things in a big way and understands how to use his abilities to adjust to the physical laws of life and demonstrate esoteric wisdom. He might become an executive in financial affairs, be a foreign ambassador, or learn how to function in a leadership role in a large organization and handle money well for the benefit of large groups of people.

His Soul Number, 5, means he has the potential to claim the right of freedom and not allow limitations on his ideals or ways of thinking. Travel— whether brief or long—contributes to his personal growth.

John's Outer Personality Number, 3, indicates he is charming and sociable. As an avid conversationalist, he shines in the midst of a group; however, there is the possibility it could cause his downfall through jealousy and conceit.

John's Path of Destiny Number, 8, indicates he has courage and stamina and can reach his goals through his own efforts. Recognition, success, executive status, and wealth are his destiny, which calls for perseverance in his career and long hours of work. He will need to learn to handle power, authority, and money optimally, as material matters must be balanced with spiritual pursuits to attain self-mastery. The arena of sports is another possibility, since this number bestows great strength and endurance.

You might have noticed that John's full name does not include the numbers 3, 7, and 9. *Missing numbers* in a person's name indicate areas that must be developed in one's lifetime. Since John does not have a 3 in his name, he needs to learn to express himself through developing his communication skills with an optimistic attitude. Traveling and broadening his mind will help with this. Lack of a 7 points to his need to develop his intuitive and philosophical side. Studying metaphysics and religion as well as meditating will be of help. Lack of a 9 also denotes he needs to become a humanitarian whose primary concern is for others. He must become an example to others through compassion and spiritually inspiring others.

As abstract as this may seem, when I had a numerology reading some time ago (based on my birth name: Jeannette Marie Hoelting), I was impressed by how descriptive it was of my personality and my life.

My Life Lesson Number is the master number 11, indicating:

- I have come into a unique and testing incarnation that involves altruism and community—decidedly ant endeavors. Although loving my neighbor as myself is a lesson to be learned, in my case, learning to love myself needed to be learned first, which involved a spider time.
- I have a strong intuition, which can be of help since the number 11 is one of the most difficult vibrations, because the need for high standards is constant.
- I must find balance between the material/physical aspects of life and the inspirational/spiritual aspects of life, which underlie my self- understanding.
- Success in a scientific field appeals to me, as well as teaching or writing. With creative flair, I could become an inspirational speaker.
- The number 11 is an esoteric master number that bestows courage, power, and talent, with strong feelings of leadership. It is important I realize that true mastery services the community.

The vowels in my name, representing my Soul Number, add up to 5—the same as John—which means I claim the right to freedom and do not allow limitations of my ideals or ways of thinking. I welcome change and engage in an assortment of ways of expressing myself.

My Outer Personality Number is 62, which reduces to 8, signifying that I am dynamic and emanate personal power and strength and tend to be ethical and impartial. I have a great deal of physical stamina and endurance.

I have no missing numbers in my name. This bodes well, especially in regard to my Path of Destiny Number: 104, which reduces to 5 and indicates many changes in my life. This requires me to willingly accept these changes to progress in my life. To quote Faith Javane and Dusty Bunker from their book *Numerology and the Divine Triangle* (1979) regarding number 5:

You are definitely not keyed to the old order or to outworn principles and ideas. You are willing to adopt new concepts and new points of understanding, even to the extent of daring to claim the liberty of suggesting new ways of doing things, and you have the ability to present the new in logical and acceptable terms. You make steppingstones of changes and cleverly turn them into growth experiences. You do not, however, forget conventions, since you are really not a rebel. Instead, you propose new ideas to promote enlightenment; you have the courage and willingness to let go of the old and experiment with the new. You are very fluent and expressive with words and could find lecturing, writing, or selling the perfect outlet for these talents (p. 34).

This description fits me—the books I've written combine the past, present, and future, with focus on pursuing personal and professional growth and change. In addition, my writing embraces both scientific and non-scientific information, with strong emphasis on spirituality.

Based on the foregoing, you too can easily identify your four personal numbers. To understand the meanings of these numbers and more, you can consult Javane and Bunker's book or many other enlightened texts.

Astrology

Regarding astrology, there are two branches: Vedic and Western. Vedic astrology, originating in India, has been practiced for thousands of years with the earliest writings found in the ancient spiritual texts of the Hindus. They observed celestial bodies that reflect their energy and light upon the Earth, therefore influencing the course of human events. Vedic astrology interpretations of a person's chart (which maps the positions of heavenly bodies at the time of birth) describe a person's psychological nature and are most often more precise than Western astrology, as they give a better view of a person's karmic tendencies (karma referring to cycles of existence) and when such tendencies are likely to manifest for that person. Western astrology also focuses on the psychological nature of the person, but lacks reliability in predicting future cycles and events.

I had an astrological reading prior to the time of replenishing myself, and I was amazed how it provided such an accurate portrayal of my personality, challenges I encountered, and aspirations I worked toward. These first readings were done by astrologers from the Western perspective, which helped me understand facets of my personality and how to use that information in beneficial ways. What follows is a Vedic description of major planetary placements in my astrological chart, which demonstrates the nature of an astrology reading and some of the factors taken into consideration.

1. A 1994 reading of my birth chart indicated how the **relationship between the sun and moon** sets a lifetime theme. Because I was born just before a full moon, my life is about a personal vision quest. When I am in phase with this quest, i.e., in synchrony, I function in harmony with my personal destiny, which involves: a passionate pursuit for an ideal sense of myself; remaining faithful to my personal discipline; being released from conventional and social responsibilities during spider times; and seeing my personal destiny as the most important driving force in my life. When out of phase, I try to be something I am not, which can entail confused self-brutality as well as deep sadness. (Although I have never physically harmed

myself, I have judged myself as not being worthy of positive manifestations in my life.)

Being in phase offers an opportunity for enjoying life with a spirit of conquest. At times I feel a strong urgency to follow a course of action, and I may abandon everything or everyone around me to pursue my goal. When I have a moment of creativity or of being triumphant, I will feel content.

Yet if I make my goal about helping the collective or addressing larger social issues or focusing on other people's maladies, this throws me out of phase. It seems I must keep my own destiny as the goal, and on that path I am able to help others, and as I do so for myself, I do it for everyone—a gift for all—an indirect result of my quest.

Recognizing universal connections in particular permeates any creative work I do, as is evident in the books I write and why they have a powerful impact on people. Reflecting on this information, I realized that it wasn't until I was middle-aged that I began to pursue my personal quest—after my children were grown and I lived alone, when I was free of others' expectations and constraints. It was then that I studied shamanism and changed the direction of my life.

2. My sun is in Pisces, and since Pisces is the last of the twelve zodiac signs, it is said to contain aspects of each sign. Consequently, Piscean individuals may seem changeable and appear not to have a singular identity. They are spiritual, dreamy, perceptive, impressionable, and artistic and can sense emotional currents within themselves and between people. Their compassionate natures can also be self-sacrificing when helping others, which can result in being taken advantage of. It is very important Pisceans develop good boundaries in their relationships with others.

Piscean creativity, however, requires self-discipline if that creativity is to be manifested. Since they are dreamers, they may live in a world of illusions and succumb to alcohol and drug abuse. When thinking about this information, I realized during my childhood I had spiritual inclinations, daydreamed considerably, and played various musical instruments. I relished taking hikes and carried a bird book to identify the many birds I spotted. By high-school years, I knew once I graduated I would move to a city. One week after graduation, I boarded the train that ran through the town and began a new life in Wisconsin, where I worked in resorts during summertime and attended college the rest of the year. Fortunately alcohol and drug abuse were not factors in my life, since I observed first hand from numerous relatives who were alcoholics the harmful results of such abuse.

3. **My moon in Virgo** indicates a need for structure, organization, and attention to detail. Combining practicality with analytical approaches helps achieve desired results. Since Virgo is a sign of service, I am apt to have an innate need to nurture myself and others through service in everyday ways. Following a healthy regimen is integral and includes exercising and solitary walks to clear the mind, along with writing in a journal so that mind, body, and spirit feel refreshed. From my experience, moon in Virgo is a needed practical complement to my dreamy sun-in-Pisces nature.

4. **My ascendant with its Saturn influence** bestows other benefits. Astrologically, the rising sign (ascendant) is specific to the time and place of birth and represents the environmental conditioning of childhood that may influence a person. It is considered as important as the sun and moon signs. The ascendant is said to be the mask one wears in public—the first impression made in meeting new people.

My chart shows a Saturn placement in Pisces, which works to pierce veils of illusion. This helps me uncover the subconscious dynamics that give rise to fears and resulting anguish. Overall, Virgo and Saturn influences are grounding and help counteract the pull of Piscean illusion. Obviously, during the time of replenishing myself, veils of illusion were uncovered that involved facing fears, terror, anxiety, and many miseries.

Of relevance is the influence of specific planets in my chart at the time of the reading. An astrologer who interprets charts both from a Western and Vedic perspective has done several readings, providing me with a perspective for the latter part of my life. These readings showed many elements in my chart coming to fruition, and it was suggested I begin to see clients again to share what I have—who I am and my inner work, which helps me feel more content. This is also a good time to further the effects of Venus being on my ascendant in Capricorn by choosing ways I can bring more beauty in my life—for example, flowers in my home, the clothes and jewelry I choose to wear.

My astrological chart also shed light on my shadow self, revealing Saturn squaring my moon in March 2015 for a year's duration, with the potential to trigger fear, terror, and anxiety. I was prepared to remedy this by feeling the terror and being with it in a Zen-like way and by journeying or meditating.

The benefits of these readings were crucial, in that they supported opportunities of connecting with others; awakening a new self; and connecting to the unknown. The astrologer rightfully referred to this time as that of transformation. My astrology readings brought focus to restructuring and accepting that I am a highly unusual person. They bolstered my courage to be with an emotion, such as terror, and to transform it with awareness.

The astrologer noted how my work and well-being are coming together and then asked how I felt about this in my physical body. I told him I feel it in my pelvis, to which he responded that such feelings in my pelvis constitute a perfect description of how this positivity manifests. He advised that when I allow pleasurable feelings, I will attract situations that support me. People will feel the spiritual riches of my writing. Venus helps me radiate this out—with heart opening and the feelings in my pelvis, along with spiritual beauty and presence in my body. This is not about overt sexual pleasure but about feeling the power centered in my pelvis. Chapter 9 will explore these issues in greater details.

An updated reading in March 2016 predicted additional areas of growth that are currently manifesting in my life:

- A deepening sense of purpose is unfolding with stability and endurance; An underpinning of expressions of love and beauty in my life and communications;
- Clarity about myself and understanding what works and what doesn't; and
- Possibly letting go of relationships that don't support me.

In addition, according to my Vedic chart, in May 2016 I began a Ketu subperiod that lasts until June 2017. Ketu influences include:

- Spiritual ideas that are out of the ordinary will be easier to write about.
- Healing for my digestive system by believing in my dreams, all of which is related to my sense of self. Yoga and Qigong will further this.
- Also of help will be not succumbing to fear.
- It is possible a new relationship will occur including Tantric sex.

Solar return occurred in March 2016, with Jupiter in my third house with a T square in Saturn, supporting:

- My writing and teaching; and

- My need to deal with identity, which involves a life review and receiving helpful information. I will find a sense of self through experiencing and identifying myself as a spiritual teacher and being an advocate for uplifting consciousness.

Astrology readings are complex and detailed; there is more I could say about what my charts revealed. Taken together with numerology, both the astrological and numerological information present a complementary picture of life—numerological from a definitive perspective and astrological from an evolutionary viewpoint. Both indicate uniqueness, courage, and spirituality.

I Ching

The I Ching originated in China and is also known as the *Book of Changes*, regarded by many to be one of the most important books of all time. Its origin goes back to mythical antiquity, with its influence inspiring three thousand years of Chinese cultural history. The two branches of Chinese philosophy, Confucianism and Taoism, have common roots here. At the outset, this book was a collection of linear signs used as oracles in response to yes/no questions. The answer *yes* was shown by an unbroken line (—) and *no* by a broken line (- -). Over time, the signs were combined in more differentiating ways, which resulted in eight trigrams that were considered images of what happens on heaven and on earth. The information transmitted now extended beyond simple yes/no questions because of the need for greater differentiation. Moreover, these symbols were considered to be in a state of ongoing transition, just as what naturally happens in the earthly world.

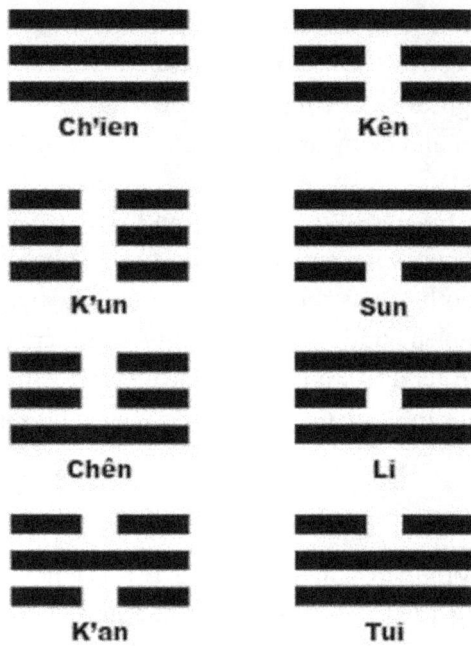

Original users consulted the I Ching by sorting yarrow stalks. Yarrow is a sacred plant permeated with spiritual power and thus appropriate for seeking the truth. As the I Ching became more widely known, the use of three coins came into being. To consult this oracle, one should think carefully about the issue and one's feelings about it and then focus on what really needs to be known. Is it an attitude, behavior, or opportunity? Questions might be:

- *What stands in the way of me succeeding at . . . ?*
- *What do I need to consider in my relationship with . . . ?*
- *What should I do about my anger in regard to . . . ?*

It is advised to write the chosen question down. Then the three coins are thrown together a number of times to make a complete hexagram. The reading of the hexagram is a complex process, and one can learn more about this via various I Ching websites.

An example of consulting the I Ching would be the situation of a teenager in his junior year of high school who, during grade-school years, had begun to play several musical instruments. Although he had above-average intelligence, he was not drawn to continuing formal education. He consulted the I Ching with the question: "What do I need to consider in pursuing a musical career?" Much to his amazement and delight, he received the first hexagram: Ch'ien (the creative/heaven), which is made up of six unbroken lines. These unbroken lines signify primal power. According to the I Ching text: "The CREATIVE works sublime success, furthering through perseverance"; and "The movement of HEAVEN is full of power. Thus the superior man makes himself strong and untiring" (*The I Ching or Book of Changes*, Richard Wilhelm, 1950, p. 4 and p. 6, respectively). Indeed, even though this individual encountered many and various challenges along the way, his commitment was strong and untiring, and he became a renowned musician whose performances occur worldwide.

Another example can be found in a novel written by Andrea Adler entitled *Pushing Upward*. The twenty-one-year-old protagonist engaged in a spiritual quest. Anguished by her childhood that had included an extremely dysfunctional family and sexual abuse, she was plagued by an eating disorder. Nonetheless, her search for meaning in life resulted from the lessons acquired from confronting the demons of her past, which involved both triumphs and challenges. Her open mind, her tenacious spirit, and her ability to let go of the past were all influenced by the I Ching—readings that helped her understand the importance of acknowledging her emotions. The wisdom of the reading of the I Ching helped in the reshaping of her life. It is obvious that Adler, as the author of this book, had a knowledgeable and experienced relationship with the I Ching.

Of note, in the foreword to Richard Wilhelm's *I Ching* book (Wilhelm, 1950), Carl Jung wrote the following:

> The I Ching does not offer itself with proofs and results; it does not vaunt itself; nor is it easy to approach. Like a part of nature it waits to be discovered. It offers neither facts nor power, but for lovers of self- knowledge, of wisdom—if there be such—it seems to be the right book. To one person its spirit appears as clear as day; to another shadowy as twilight; to a third dark as night. He who is not pleased by it does not have to use it, and he who is against it is not obliged to find it true. Let it go forth into the world for the benefit of those who can discern its meaning (p. xxxix).

My experience of using the I Ching was somewhat brief, since I often found the hexagrams difficult to interpret. In discovering the runes, I found an oracle more suited to my need for more understandable readings. A book entitled *Way of Council Ancient Wisdom* by Jack Zimmerman and Virginia Coyle presents a streamlined and easier way to consult the I Ching.

Runes

Ralph Blum, who researched and authored *The Book of Runes*, was a graduate of Harvard, a Fulbright Scholar, and a cultural anthropologist. As described in the preface of this book (Blum, 1993), using the runes involves consulting an oracle rather than having your fortune told.

> An oracle does not give you instruction as what to do next, nor does it predict future events. An oracle points your attention toward those hidden fears and motivations that will shape your future by their unfelt presence within each moment. Once seen and recognized, these elements become absorbed

into the realm of choice. Oracles do not absolve you of the responsibility for selecting your future but rather direct your attention toward those inner choices that may be the most important elements in determining that future (p. 8).

Runes are characters in the alphabet used in ancient times by people of northern Europe. Blum further states that the Runes are: "An ancient alphabetic script, each of whose letters posed a meaningful name as well as a signifying sound. Runes were employed for legal documents, for writing poetry, for inscriptions and divination, yet never evolved as a spoken language" (p. 12).

Originally there were twenty-four runes, with the blank rune added by Blum. An exemplary use of the runes occurred when Blum consulted this oracle regarding the timeliness of writing his book. Using the three-rune spread, he drew:

- Ingus, the rune of fertility and new beginnings, reflecting the timeliness of writing;
- Nauthiz, the rune of constraint, necessity, and pain, which indicates there may well be holdups and reasons to delay plans—appropriate advice for any undertaking; and in Blum's case, reflected the many of hours of writing, editing, and reworking parts of the book—all not without pain; and
- Dagaz, the rune of breakthrough and transformation, indicating self- change will occur, which involves a complete change in attitude with fertile and fruitful outcomes.

Drawing a single rune can be helpful when an overview of a situation is wanted; when stressful conditions occur; and to honor significant life events, such as solstices, equinoxes, deaths, births, anniversaries, birthdays, and other important occasions. I have found the runes to be a trusted and valid resource for many life issues—from pointing out aspects of my shadow self to indicating how to advance in a spiritual manner. Recording rune readings in my journal is of great benefit.

Tarot

Many varieties of tarot card decks exist, and there is no standard number of cards. Decks have various themes including nature, animals, fantasy, dragons, and others. The most common deck in the United Sates is the Rider- Waite, whose popularity and longevity is credited to the colorful illustrations on the cards.

The tarot deck is made up of the minor arcana and major arcana cards. The minor arcana cards include four suits: wands, swords, cups, and circles (or pentacles). The cards within these suits are numbered one through ten and include the king, queen, knight, and page. Each suit has a meaning regarding a specific approach to life and represents the more minor, practical occurrences in daily life.

The major arcana cards signify strong, long-term energy or large events in some area of life. They include picture cards that present principles, concepts, and ideals and are numbered one through twenty-one. The twenty-second card (named the fool card) is marked as zero. Drawing a major arcana card about a specific issue in one reading and then drawing a minor arcana card about the same issue in the following reading means this issue is becoming less important in your life.

A person can become a tarot card reader by studying books and taking courses. One can even become certified by the American Board for Tarot certification, which offers five levels of certification.

What's for You?

Consulting oracles varies from individual to individual and does not appeal to everyone. Some choose one they consistently rely on, while others prefer a combination. Numerology provides fixed information about one's character, including strengths and weaknesses. Astrology, while not being an oracle per se, presents information according to where planets are located in a person's chart, with changes constantly occurring as the planets rotate. The Runes, I Ching, and Tarot are used to obtain information about problems and events occurring in one's life and how best to process them and benefit from the situations being encountered.

Even if the idea of consulting oracles seems alien to you, consider experimenting with one or two of them. Oracles provide information and insights into behaviors and attitudes that can promote positive shifts and changes in one's life. The reason I am writing this book and you are reading it is that both you and I want to achieve as much emotional and spiritual maturity as possible while helping to heal the entire planet!

WORKS CITED

Adler, A. (2012). *Pushing upward.* Carlsbad, CA: Hay House. Amen, D. G. (2013). *Unleash the power of the female brain: Supercharging yours for better health, energy, mood, focus and sex.* New York: Harmony Books.

Blum, R. H. (1993). *Book of the runes.* New York: St. Martin's Press. Gagan, J. M. (2014). *Grow up your ego: Ten scientifically validated stages to emotional and spiritual maturity.* Santa Fe, NM: Rio Chama Publications.

Janvane, F. & Bunker, D. (1979). *Numerology and the divine triangle.* Chester, PA: Whitford Press.

Jung, C.J. (1967). *Symbols of transformation* (2nd ed.) in *The collected works*, vol. 5. Bollingen Series, XX, trans. R.F.C. Hull. Princeton, NJ: Princeton University Press.

Wilhelm, R. (trans.) (1950). *The I Ching or book of changes: The Richard Wilhelm Translation*, Bollingen Series XIX. New York: Princeton University Press.

Vaillant, G. E. (1993). *The wisdom of the ego*. Cambridge, MA: Harvard University Press.

Weil, A. (1995). *Spontaneous healing*. New York: Knopf. Zimmerman, J. & Coyle, V. (2009). *Way of council ancient wisdom*. Colchester, United Kingdom: Bramble Books.

Chapter 7

Mentors And Non-Mentors

I MENTIONED MENTORS IN Chapter 6 among those who can provide a nurturing, accepting environment that helps us grow. Such pairings fall between solitary spider work and broader ant-like collaborations. A mentor is an experienced and trusted person who shares their knowledge with others. Throughout life we encounter many—from grade-school teachers to individuals who advise us about problematic situations, be they in the family, workplace, social settings, creative endeavors, or elsewhere. In reviewing my life with mentors in mind, I was pleasantly surprised by the various ways this occurred.

On the other hand, a non-mentor is a person who withholds knowledge from others or may share inappropriate information and exhibit inappropriate behaviors. Such disconnections can happen frequently in male-female encounters, across all walks of life, especially when there is an imbalance of energies and power. Awareness of these problems is growing, and we can hope future generations will encounter them less and less. Unlike mentors, whose influence is empowering, non-mentors leave their victims feeling exploited, vulnerable, stupid, or powerless.

Sexual misconduct of non-mentors occurs frequently. When I was in graduate school pursuing a PhD in psychology, all the professors were male. One in particular had a reputation for seducing female students—never mind that he was married. I was not a student in any of his classes, but I was aware of the problem. As this kind of behavior violates psychological ethics to the maximum, it was especially egregious.

Similarly, most of us are aware that some spiritual leaders abuse their influence and position, whether it is to satisfy their greed or lust. It matters little if their group is a conventional religion or a cult or a yoga practice. Sexual misconduct cannot be tolerated in educational, military, workplace, or family relationships.

Other common characteristics of non-mentors include disrespect and dominance. My experience with medical doctors in an adversarial way first occurred when I was a student nurse at a hospital in the 1950s. The doctor who delivered the most babies was known for treating women in labor with "twilight sleep"—a popular approach at the time. This combination of analgesia (pain relief) and amnesia (loss of memory), produced by a mixture of morphine and scopolamine, would be given by hypodermic injection under the skin. Unknown to most people outside the medical environment, this resulted in women thrashing irrationally, banging their heads, and experiencing hallucinations. Even though they did feel pain, due to the amnesia they did not remember it. Patients were known to stand up in the bed and say nonsensical things and sometimes had to be tied down. When the delivery happened, they sometimes weren't aware of it and were surprised when they were shown the baby that had been delivered. Given what we know today about the importance of early, consistent maternal holding, this is obviously a harmful way for a child to begin life, not to mention robbing the mother of such an important experience.

In contrast, another obstetrician on the staff advocated natural childbirth. I witnessed many such deliveries as a student. Often the pregnant mothers attended classes in which they learned breathing exercises that would help them relax during contractions. This helps the baby as well, since the mother is not struggling with or resisting pain.

When I was married and pregnant with my first child, this was the doctor I went to. I had a long labor during which I did breathing exercises. When my cervix was dilated—initiating the second stage of labor during which the fetus moves down through the birth canal—the doctor was called. The second stage lasted three hours; for some women, it can last a matter of minutes. The doctor sat patiently with me throughout the entire three hours, coaching and applauding as progress was made. A local anesthetic was given.

Subsequent pregnancies and deliveries differed because we lived in various locations, none of which seemed to have obstetricians who promoted natural childbirth. They used epidural injections (a numbing medication) into the spinal column. In one delivery I told the obstetrician I wanted to have a pudendal block, to which he responded he wasn't experienced at giving them. Nonetheless he administered it, which only anesthetized half of my perineum, vulva, and vagina. Even though I felt some pain, it was an ecstatic experience because I was feeling the naturalness of this event—physically and emotionally—which is often described as an "ultimate orgasm," as the mother feels the baby moving through the birth canal and delivered into life.

In another delivery, as I lay on the delivery table and told the doctor I did not want any anesthetic, he replied, "The Model-T Ford went out of style in the 1920s," meaning I was out of touch with modern life in choosing pain over relief. Little did he know what I and others are capable of experiencing when delivery is natural. In my last pregnancy and delivery, I gave up trying to convince the obstetrician I could handle a natural childbirth with no or very little anesthetic.

Mentors

Marge

One of my earliest mentors was my oldest sister, Marge. Her guidance influenced my growth educationally and professionally, and I chose to move near her and her husband in Milwaukee to attend Marquette University. On weekends when I visited them, Marge helped me with homework, as I found the challenge of my freshman year somewhat overwhelming, having graduated from a small-town high school that did not include preparatory classes for college.

Marge was a registered nurse who worked as a supervisor in a long-term care facility where death was a frequent visitor. She had read and shared with me Elisabeth Kubler-Ross's book, *On Grief and Grieving*, which exposed the sad truth of how dying patients are often ignored. As a psychiatrist, Dr. Kubler-Ross was the perfect person to author such a book, since she did extensive research by spending time and talking with dying patients. In her book she described the five stages of grief:

1. denial—shutting oneself off from others and refusing to accept the reality of what is happening;
2. anger—"Why me?" and the need to blame;
3. bargaining—"If this weren't happening, I would do this or that";
4. depression—feeling there is no reason to go on and feeling overwhelmed; and
5. acceptance—accepting what is.

When Marge (a nonsmoker) had a routine physical exam at age forty-nine, a tumor was discovered in one of her lungs; it was surgically removed. Even though the tumor was malignant, it was said to be localized and she was given a good prognosis. However, about a year later, she woke one morning and discovered she was paralyzed from her breasts down. The cancer had metastasized to her spine. In addition to her husband giving her physical care, home health aides were hired throughout the day. She lived for almost a year in this condition, and as death drew closer she was taken to the hospital.

I traveled on the train from Santa Fe to the Midwest and visited her.

Fortunately she was conscious, and as I sat at her bedside, she told me it was a comfort to have me present, as she felt safe with me. She described how, when neighbors and friends visited her, they didn't know what to say and kept their visits short. Marge remembered when our mother died, everything was secret—no one mentioned she was dying, and we children were left to wonder what was occurring. Marge chose to share with her husband and children the reality of her last months and days of her life, which was very beneficial to their grieving process.

Marge knew I was no longer Catholic and pursued other spiritual paths, of which she was very accepting. She asked if we could pray together—first Catholic prayers and then some prayers from a book I had with me that were more Buddhist-like. When it was time for me to leave, she said she felt sad, as she so appreciated me sitting with her. I told her that when she missed me, to bring me into her awareness and feel my presence with her, to which she agreed. As I slept on the train ride home, I woke around 4:00 a.m. and felt her presence with me, which was comforting. On disembarking from the train, I was given the news Marge had died about that time in the morning.

The sum of this is that Marge both helped guide my early adult choices and also widely broadened my understanding of the intricacies of death and dying. In the last year of her life, even though I don't know to what degree she experienced the five stages of loss, I do know in the end she modeled a peaceful death to me.

In the hospital setting

Death and dying are universally difficult stages of life that few learn to accept. In addition to Marge, I encountered other mentors in this important area.

After graduating from college, I took a position as a staff nurse at the Milwaukee Veterans Administration Hospital, working on a large ward where several patients were dying. Two patients and the head nurse taught me a great deal. One patient, Mr. D, was dying of cancer, in a ward that had eight beds. When staff entered the ward, it was very evident how Mr. D, in spite of his pain, was at peace with himself and his upcoming death. In fact, a glow seemed to emanate from him as he cheerfully greeted each person. I was amazed by his calm and accepting demeanor, which I have never forgotten; he taught me that one can die with peace in one's heart.

The other patient who was dying was in a private room and struggled immensely with his pain and coming demise. He was rude and impatient with staff, except for the head nurse, Ms. Anderson, who when time permitted sat at his bedside and extended her loving presence to him in silence. This taught me how important it is that no matter what a dying person may be experiencing, expressing, or not expressing, one need not avoid or run away from such a situation but can accept it exactly as it is. When Ms. Anderson sat with this patient, he indeed was calmer and did not act out in her presence.

Elisabeth Kubler-Ross

It may seem paradoxical that I place such importance on "death" mentoring, but of course death and life are intimately intertwined. After Marge's death, I attended an Elisabeth Kubler-Ross week-long workshop in California. She explained how the five stages apply to other losses in life as well, and said that each of us would have the opportunity to work on a specific loss in our lives. One by one, we stood in the center of the room and described our loss in detail, allowing whatever feelings occurred to be expressed, be it crying or anger—for the latter, a foot-long rubber hose was available as well as a mattress.

When it was my turn, I began to describe how I had been lied to and betrayed by a colleague whom I had asked to write a letter of reference for me. Even though he assured me he always wrote positive reference letters, I later learned his letter was negative. As I felt rage stirring within me, I picked up the rubber hose and began beating it on the mattress while yelling out my rage. Never before in my life had I allowed such strong emotion to be expressed, yet I knew this emotion was in me and needed to be released within this safe and caring environment—just as Marge shared her experiences of dying with me in the safety of our relationship. As a result of my experience, I understood how rage is a natural reaction and emotion to betrayals and abuse. I then purchased a rubber hose that I used in the privacy of my home when such rage surfaced. This provided an ongoing benefit of knowing I was not helpless and could accept and express my own violent emotions without harming myself or others.

L.C. Smith

In the 1960s I served as county chairman of Project Understanding, a volunteer organization that promoted equality and understanding between races. Founded by a law student, this organization's activities brought African American children from rural Mississippi to Wisconsin counties, where they stayed in Caucasian homes for several weeks. My counterpart in Mississippi was a remarkable black man named L.C. Smith. Not only did he accompany the children on the bus that brought them to Wisconsin, he also came during the school year to speak at school assemblies about the reality of being a black person in the southern states of this country.

On the occasion that my husband and I traveled on the train to Mississippi, L.C. drove us in his car around the county—an unheard of event for a black man to be driving two white people in an old vehicle. It was no surprise but still shocking to learn that L.C. was a target of the Ku Klux Klan. Yet this did not deter him from continuing with his responsibilities as the chairman of Project Understanding. L.C. and his wife had eight children, and during our visit to their house—best described as a shack with no electricity or plumbing—L.C. sat and spoke with us about the importance of healing race relations and improving the abysmal conditions of poverty in which many African Americans lived.

Listening to the passion and compassion of this man for the betterment of humankind, amid such poverty and daily threats to his life, deeply affected my husband and me. Instead of being bitter and feeling defeated, L.C. envisioned a better life for his family and other people and did everything he could to further that in a non-violent way. What I learned from this man was the importance of knowing one's truth and creating resourceful ways of pursuing it. He also modeled how female power can so effectively exist with male expression.

Two Professors

My own passion is expressed through a number of pursuits—obviously writing being a major one. In the mid-1970s I attended a creative writing class taught by an award-winning author. Students were instructed to write short fictional stories. One story I wrote, entitled "The Boat of Three Happy Ladies" (inspired by a painting), described how three ladies during the night would visit specific individuals in their dreams and offer suggestions for solving some of their life dilemmas. The professor especially liked this story and encouraged me to continue writing.

Although I didn't maintain interest in writing fiction, the fruits of what I had learned stood me in good stead when I entered graduate school in the late-1970s and fulfilled course assignments through the written word. One of the professors drew attention to the ability I have of writing about an issue from various perspectives, which is especially important when doing research. She encouraged me to expand this ability in my master's thesis and in my doctoral dissertation as well as to write and submit articles to professional journals—some of which were published. I not only found this approach natural and enjoyable, it enriched the books I've written.

My Intuition

Though it may seem odd, I regard my intuition as a mentor: it guided me along my path of spiritual growth. One prime example of this was in 1992, when my intuition led me to pursue a visit of several month's duration in South America. This trip constituted my first experience of being in countries that, at the time, had many economic and political hardships and challenges. Prior to this, I had traveled only in the United States and northern Europe.

When I first arrived in Ecuador, for a number of weeks I attended classes to learn Spanish. The instructor thought I would quickly learn the language since he knew I had a PhD. However, much to his and my dismay, my brain didn't seem to be wired for learning a new language. If there had been a dunce hat available, I would have been the one to wear it!

Furthermore, I had lodging with a local family whose use of the English language was limited. I related well to the father and two children, but the mother was an alcoholic and, when drunk, would yell at family members. Often I remained in my room. This experience was a disappointment.

Toward the end of my stay, though, I signed up for a trip to Peru, followed by a trip to the Galapagos, and fortunately the guide spoke English. The trip to Peru was indeed memorable, as we visited Machu Picchu even though the Shining Path—a group of Maoist guerrillas—was active in the area and perpetrated assassinations, bombings, and beheadings. In fact, prior to the trip, travelers were told this would be the last trip this organization would schedule due to acceleration of Shining Path activity.

On arrival at Machu Picchu, to my surprise I did not feel fear; I was so taken by the beauty and spiritual nature of this wonder of the world. Visiting the Galapagos carried a magic of its own. These islands are sanctuaries where animals and birds live in a natural way. Each day a guide would accompany our group of about ten on walks, with the understanding we were to stay on the trails to ensure the environment would not be damaged. A highlight of the trip was swimming with the seals in the ocean—an exquisite and delightful experience as the seals swam next to me.

On my return to the United States, I was contacted by a woman I had met in South America, who lived in the Midwest. She informed me that a Medicine Woman would be coming to Santa Fe to give a retreat, and since she planned to attend, she suggested I do so also. This was a fortuitous occurrence since after the retreat I met with the Medicine Woman in private, and she blew my first power animal into me—an initiation into my shamanic training and heritage, as she explained the animal was a teacher and would activate my teaching abilities.

Even though I did not encounter the Medicine Woman again, I embarked on the shamanic path and attended trainings from the Foundation for Shamanic Studies. As you know by now, this has been a keystone to my life and my life's work.

Twylah Nitsch

When I learned of a shamanic elder named Twylah Nitsch, I contacted her and asked if I could do an apprenticeship with her, to which she agreed. In 1993 when I flew to Buffalo, New York, close to the reservation where she lived, I was met by one of her staff, who drove us through pouring rain in the late evening to Twylah's home. Since Twylah went to sleep early, I was given a bed in a small upstairs room, where I comfortably slept. The next day and following days, Twylah spent many hours telling me her life history and sharing the teachings of her shamanic heritage. Totally fascinated and feeling very blessed, I soaked in as much information as I could.

The bond that developed between us continued after I returned home, and we periodically spoke on the phone as well as exchanged letters. When I finished writing the *Journeying* book, I sent her an unpublished version, requesting an endorsement. She wrote: "This phenomenal book . . . shows how the separating and controlling energy of violence transforms into healing unity. This is 'must reading' as we work toward a world of illumination and cooperation for the coming millennium."

Specifically, my relationship with Twylah was not only a mentoring one but also one in which she emphasized how, even though I was not a Native American or born into a family with known shamanic heritage, that in this lifetime I am remembering and reactivating this heritage from other lifetimes.

In 1996 a tape I received from Twylah emphasized how entering into silence—as in meditation—involves identifying and experiencing spiritual wants and expressions of gratitude. This is what she said about meditating:

> As I enter my truth I use my silence to concentrate on my Earth Path through love, truth, and peace.
>
> I enter deeper into the silence to my within—love; my within—truth; my within—peace.
>
> I enter deeper into the silence through cause, truth, and affect.
>
> I enter deeper into the silence through thoughts and actions and as a regulator/truth refiner. I approach my alignment of silent stillness.

Next Twylah listed seven gratitudes:

1. Connection with the divine
2. Healthy body that I love
3. Strengthening intuition for teaching and service
4. Strengthening seeing to be the seer/motivator
5. Expanding creativity to be the worker/creator
6. Strengthening/honoring to be the assessor/appraiser for principle and a code of ethics
7. Deepening listening to be the listener/thinker

In her own voice she concluded with these words:

> Through my silence I synthesize all these components into wholeness, and I am recharged as a crystal light. My inner sight is awakened to my vibral core—the source of the real me. I see the field of plenty shimmering before me through silent stillness. I draw it toward me and as it flows over my head—surrounding, assisting, filtering, screening, and draping me into its wholeness—I transcend into the unity of my physicality and spirituality. As my boundary encircles my wholeness, I thank the great mystery, my band members, and my ancient ancestors with all my relations. My body is now healed, refreshed, restored, and enlightened. I now nestle into sleep, into silence—silent stillness where truth is my wholeness.

Twylah died in 2007, and prior to her death she wrote these words to me:

> I am gathering twelve people together: six men and six women. Yes, you are one of the women. The Wheel I have drawn on this page represents the Cycles of Truth. I still recall my grandparents

reminding me that: "Truth is our Watchword. Truth is our Key. Truth is our Password. Truth sets us Free."

I have not yet met the other eleven people. The last years of Twylah's life seem to have been for her a spider time. She was a strong warrioress of truth, which I have reflected on a great deal. Along with the word *know* (she used the word *know* in reference to me), I learned from Twylah that it was my mission to seek truth, to own that I know it, and to teach it to others—all a manifestation of shamanic heritage. During my current writings regarding feminine energy, I often think that Twylah is smiling down on me, helping me to share the knowing and truth of who I am so that others might be inspired to pursue the same enlightenment.

Author Margaret Wolff's book, *In Sweet Company: Conversations with Extraordinary Women about Living a Spiritual Life* (2004), describes many details of Twylah's life, including when the Dalai Lama visited Twylah in her home in the winter of 1991. During their conversations they talked about international situations and shared thoughts about their desires for world peace. Then as they walked arm in arm along the snow-covered path to the Wolf Clan Lodge, they slid on a patch of ice and fell on their backs into the snow. Laughing as they got up, each gathered a lump of snow and started a snowball fight.

Twylah was blessed with ancient wisdom that she readily shared with others. I am very grateful for her presence in my life and what she imparted to me. Since her death, I experience times of feeling her close to me— sometimes in dreams and especially when I do a shamanic journey.

Mother Meera

In the late 1990s I traveled to Europe to attend an international book fair, where I hoped to sell foreign rights of *Journeying: Where*

Shamanism and Psychology Meet to publishers in other countries. I heard that Mother Meera, a spiritual woman from India, would be giving a Darshan (a ritual in which she touches a person's head and looks into their eyes and infuses them with light) in a German village. Immediately I boarded a train to that destination.

Mother Meera is one of the most widely revered and loved of Avatars (human incarnations of a Hindu god on earth) and is worshipped as a Divine Mother in India, where she was born in 1960. She had her first Samadhi—a state of complete spiritual absorption—when she was six years old that lasted a whole day. During the Darshan, where I sat in the room with many others to receive Mother Meera's blessing, I experienced an awareness of my mother and her sisters, which I later realized signified unfinished business I needed to deal with, emotionally and spiritually.

This of course was prior to my 2003 second sabbatical and a telling forecast. Since all my grandparents were born in Germany, and I did not bond with my mother, here in Germany I was learning what needed to be healed within me. This also occurred about the time (previously described in Chapter 2) when, in a hypnotherapy session, I experienced an elephant trying to climb the stairs from the basement to the main floor of my mother's home. Needless to say this experience was not what I anticipated, yet I have Mother Meera to thank for providing the necessary atmosphere in which I could grasp the truth of what needed to be healed.

Book Editor

When I hired the editor of my second book, she quickly became a mentor. Prior to this, I had hired several others who were deficient in one way or another. In addition to being an excellent editor and teaching me a great deal about writing, my new editor was also a published author. From our many conversations, I knew her to be an advocate for citizen rights and equality in all arenas. When I read her book, I was amazed by its accuracy and insights into slavery in America during the nineteenth century. Her purpose in writing the book was to expand readers' knowledge about race relations—a purpose she continues to pursue through a second edition of the book and discussions on her website. Consequently she has modeled to me effective and appropriate ways to write, publish, and teach others basic truths—be they psychological, philosophical, or cultural. Even when she edits material that seems "far out" (as in this book), she does so with genuine interest and non- judgment while considering what would be most relevant to readers. Her style is that of reading and listening with a discerning mind and an open heart and giving feedback in kind and gentle ways.

Brian Yee

In January of 2013 I had my first session with Brian Yee. In addition to being a massage therapist, he is a remarkable channeler of spiritual and psychological information, which is most helpful. Often at the beginning of the session before I say anything, he describes what I have been feeling, which amazes me. Then as he does energy work on me—often without touching me—he shares what is happening. Even though he never thought of himself as a shaman, his work is shamanic. Sometimes he has brought energy back into my body just as a shaman does during a soul retrieval. Other times he has removed energy from my body that didn't belong (energy I had taken on from other persons), which in shamanism is termed an *extraction*.

Never once have I felt judged by him. Rather, he explains how my experiences involved astrological and/or past- and present-life influences, while emphasizing how this is the way we human beings can progress spiritually. It is not a matter of being right or wrong but learning necessary lessons that involve choosing to change behaviors and actions in order to advance.

I increased our sessions to weekly after I finished Brain Dynamics sessions, and this was very beneficial. My experience of his work is that of providing a bridge between letting go of the past and moving into a more enlightened future. Brian modeled to me the importance and power of not judging clients while emphasizing their strengths and offering practical and grounded recommendations for moving forward both psychologically and spiritually. He is another example of men in my life who embrace their feminine power to the benefit of all.

No doubt you have experienced non-mentors and mentors in your life. You might be surprised by how beneficial it can be to make a list of them and the ways they were or were not helpful and what you learned from those experiences. Exploring how non-mentors and mentors resulted in ant- community or spider-reclusive activities in your life may deepen your understanding of their influence—whether adverse or helpful. And all efforts you make to learn from your experiences will help you mature in the best of ways.

WORKS CITED

Kubler-Ross, E. and Kessler, D. (2014). *On grief and grieving: Finding the meaning through the five stages of loss* (commemorative edition). New York: Scribner.

Wolff, M. (2004). *In sweet company: Conversations with extraordinary women about living a spiritual life*. San Francisco: Jossey-Bass.

Chapter 8

Feminine Energy in Relationships

TWYLAH NITSCH, MY mentor who was mentioned in the previous chapter, stressed the importance of "how the separating and controlling energy of violence can transform into healing unity." Many of my personal examples have reflected this, and I believe most, if not all, of us have experienced relationships with such separating and controlling energies: whether they be adult to child, spouse to spouse, lover to lover, or friend to friend partnerships. As mentioned, the ability to form true partnership is a key trait of goddesses and of feminine energy. This chapter will explain in more detail just what that means and what "balance" of masculine and feminine energies entails. I will present research results and recommendations from several perspectives that describe aspects of a successful marriage (or partnership), along with examples from my own life.

The Seven Principles of Marriage

The Seven Principles for Making Marriage Work, by John Gottman, PhD, contains information relevant to any relationship and is based on the outcomes of sound research in which the fates of couples in seven different studies were tracked for up to twenty years. At the outset, Dr. Gottman established the Love Lab at the Gottman

Institute in Seattle in 1986. This outstanding project involved fifty randomly selected couples.

One day of the weekend, a couple would spend twenty-four hours in the Love Lab in a studio apartment that had a lovely view of a lake. Three video cameras were attached to the wall, microphones were clipped to each of their collars, and Holter monitors were strapped around their chests, which provided continuous recording of each person's heartbeat via an EKG reading. Couples were told to act as they usually did; they were monitored from 9:00 a.m. to 9:00 p.m. There was a foldout sofa, kitchen, phone, television, and music player in the apartment. Couples could bring laptops, books, exercise equipment, and even their pets.

Research results of all seven projects were accurate enough that Gottman became able to predict with 91 percent accuracy whether a marriage would fail or not by listening to their interactions for fifteen minutes. What were his criteria?

- The first sign was a harsh start-up of a discussion, marked by negativity, sarcasm, and accusations.
- The second sign involved what the project termed as "the four horsemen": criticism, contempt, defensiveness, and stonewalling.
- The third sign was "emotional flooding" as a result of being psychologically and physically overwhelmed.
- The fourth sign was body language—the heart sped up at more than one hundred beats a minute, adrenalin was secreted, blood pressure spiked, and sweating occurred.

Notice in these four signs that separating and controlling energy is active. All this together resulted in an inability to pay attention and to process information, with creative problem solving and use of a sense of humor being strangers in this terrain.

In 85 percent of heterosexual marriages, the stonewaller is the male. This is related to anthropological evidence that indicates we evolved from hominids whose lives were characterized by gender roles necessary for survival. The women tended to children while the men hunted and protected. Even today the male cardiovascular system is more reactive than the female and is slower to recover from stress. Thankfully, we continue to evolve. As previously mentioned, more males are beginning to nurture children—demonstrating a positive advance in the evolutionary scheme of things.

Gottman also studied same-sex couples over twelve years and found many of the same problematic dynamics exist as with heterosexuals. Research also showed the same pathways to staying happy together and that same-sex couples tend to be more upbeat regarding conflict. They use more affect and humor, and partners are more positive in their reception of such. They also use fewer controlling, hostile emotional strategies. When engaged in conflict, negative comments are taken less personally and are less likely to produce hurt feelings, while positive comments create more good feelings and facilitate resolution. Furthermore, studies showed gay and lesbian couples demonstrate a greater ability to soothe one another, thus reducing the arousal of hostile feelings during conflict. Lesbians showed more anger, humor, excitement, and interest than their counterparts among gay men. Both gay men and lesbian women have been raised in a culture where expressiveness is more acceptable for women than for men, and this is indicated as such in their relationships (Gottman, 1999).

Gottman concluded that "repair attempts" are a happy couple's secret weapon and are used by emotionally intelligent couples. Repair attempts refer to any statement or action, whether silly or otherwise, that prevents a negative dynamic from spiraling out of control. Significantly, Gottman reported that most arguments *can't* be resolved, since most are about deeper, hidden issues that fuel superficial conflicts.

The solution is to understand the deeper cause of the conflict and learn to accept it by honoring and respecting each other. Yet exploring deeper causes of conflicts is not easy, as it entails ongoing observation of how one thinks and behaves. For example, when a wife becomes very upset because her husband spends too many evenings with his male friends, she doesn't realize how this resonates on a deeper level with her childhood experiences. Her father was an alcoholic and spent too much money and time on liquor. Afraid of him when he returned home drunk and volatile, she had to repress her anger toward him. Gaining insight into this dynamic is the first step toward repair. The second step is to communicate with her husband using an "I message," such as: "I feel lonely, fearful, and abandoned when you are out with your friends because it reminds me of when I was a child—my dad came home drunk, he was abusive. I need to be reassured that when you return from being with your friends, you will hold me in your arms and say loving things to me."

Successful partnerships involve each partner supporting the other's hopes and dreams. Toward this end, Gottman formulated the Seven Principles:

Principle #1: **Enhance your love maps**—engage and develop the part of the brain where you store all relevant information about your partner's life. Create plenty of cognitive room for the marriage. Remember major events in each other's lives and update information as changes occur; they know what the other's favorite foods are; they know how the other feels about his/her boss; they know the role spirituality and/or religion plays in the other's life; and they know each other's life goals, worries, and wishes.

Principle #2: **Nurture your fondness and admiration**—remind yourself of your spouse's positive qualities and maintain respect for her/him. Frequent verbalizing of heartfelt gratitude and appreciation for your spouse strengthens the marital bond.

Principle #3: **Turn toward each other instead of away**—connect with your partner. In marriage, spouses are constantly making bids for each other's attention—from asking for a back rub to helping with an ill relative. When partners listen, hear, and respond to each other they turn *toward* each other, which forms the basis of trust, emotional connection, passion, and a satisfying sex life.

Principle # 4: **Let your partner influence you**—both men and women can be reluctant to share their power as well as be resistant to their partner's power. However, when a husband accepts his wife's influence and when a wife acknowledges her husband's power, it strengthens their friendship. This reduces power struggles and each learns a great deal from the other.

Principle # 5: **Solve your solvable problems**—there are two kinds of conflicts: *perpetual* and *solvable*. Perpetual problems include deciding to have a baby, one spouse wants more sex than the other, and differing philosophies about childrearing. Examples of solvable problems include those that involve a particular dilemma or situation, such as driving speeds, taking garbage out, or spending inheritance money. The good news is that perpetual problems do not have to be resolved for a marriage to survive. The answer rests in learning how to cope, negotiate, and overcome gridlock.

Principle: # 6 **Overcome gridlock**—gridlock occurs when one isn't aware of, doesn't acknowledge, or doesn't respect their partner's dreams for life. This problem is addressed by detecting and discussing the dreams, taking a break from the discussion, and soothing each other. This may be indicated when conflict discussions trigger *flooding*; i.e., when one is overwhelmed emotionally and physically. The first thing to do is to end the discussion and do something soothing, such as listening to music, taking a walk, or sitting quietly in the garden. Comforting each other can occur by giving each other massages or by taking turns guiding each other through a meditation. Overcoming gridlock also involves reaching a temporary compromise, understanding there will always be a difference regarding this problem, and thanking each other and showing appreciation and gratitude for each other.

Principle # 7: **Create shared meaning**—the bottom line of a happy marriage is creating a shared meaning, which can be achieved by creating an atmosphere that encourages each person to talk honestly about his or her convictions. In doing so, a blending of each other's sense of meaning becomes more likely. Every person has a philosophy, and couples with happy marriages share their underlying purpose for being alive. Asking questions of each other—What is most important? What is the legacy you want to leave? What is your sense of purpose?—further promotes shared meaning. Although the two underlying purposes may not be the same, awareness of this inspires support and helps with loving understanding toward one another.

Constructive Communication

Solving problems is basic to any positive relationship. Too often discussions begin with "you" messages: you ignore me; you always nag. Constructive messages have three steps:

1. Begin with "I feel--" and then complete the statement with an honest statement of your feeling and a description of the behavior that triggered that feeling. For example: "I feel hurt when others don't listen to me." "I feel sad when I don't know where you are."
2. State what is needed. "I need others to give me full attention when I talk about a problematic issue." "I need to know you care for me."
3. Acknowledge your partner's feeling of hurt. If you did not know of your partner's feelings prior to this, tell the partner so while emphasizing you want to better the situation in an appropriate way. Questioning the partner to elicit more details is helpful because it lets the partner know you are

interested in addressing the situation. Also questioning the partner about what he/she thinks would help remedy the situation and indicates your sincerity. In instances when your behavior has been unsuitable say, "I'm sorry," "please forgive me," or "how can I make this up to you?"

The Esoteric Path of Marriage

Maha and David Brown, in their book *The Esoteric Path of Marriage*, present information from a spiritual perspective with the hope it will assist the evolution of consciousness on this planet. As a guidebook, it is directed toward self-realization—that is, fulfillment by oneself of the possibilities of one's character or personality. This requires that the old relationship paradigm, which was essentially patriarchal, be replaced by one in which the divine feminine and divine masculine are serving one another, both within us and within the relationship. Specifically the authors state:

> For we are all uniting in a common goal that affects us all, realizing as we do that man is not separate from his environment; we are charged with birthing a new paradigm that places man as custodian of the planet and the Life that She nurtures rather than as an errant king with the power to take whatever is there. Within this new paradigm enlightened relationships flourish. Marriage is transmuted from coming together in struggle against scarcity into coming together to transcend negativity, to perfect ourselves from the inside-out so that we are the best possible versions of ourselves. And in this relationship, space opens up for us to bring our deepest gifts to the Whole, to the planet and all of Creation (p. 12).

According to the authors, this paradigm is attainable through forging new agreements, and they list fourteen guidelines:

1. Commit your relationship to the fire of self-knowledge, which means committing to the painful task of unearthing buried emotions.
2. Your partner is not responsible for your happiness, which is the opposite of the belief that the job of one's partner is to make the mate happy. The source of one's happiness comes from within the self.
3. By the same token, you are not responsible for your partner's happiness.
4. Process your own emotional pain.
5. Let your love be unconditional by dropping all your agendas; this results from finding unconditional love for oneself as one surrenders to life and the lessons life brings.
6. Realize that your partner is not an object frozen in time and space and neither are you. Each of us is a process—formless, eternal, expanding, and evolving through matter.
7. Be aware of promises—accept that life is about change. Instead of saying, "I promise," say something like, "Let's gather more information about this issue."
8. Set a good example for your partner—honor your partner by honoring yourself and leading by example.
9. Be the first to lay down your arms—such acts of heroism provide a better chance of moving through conflicts more quickly.
10. Your partner is not yours to own—in the new paradigm, relationship is a tool for liberation, not another thing to own, control, or imprison you.
11. Your partner is holy, and so are you, because the center of the relationship is with the One Consciousness/the deepest Self.

12. Treat your partner with the same respect you would a stranger, which helps keep the relationship new and fresh.
13. You are not a safe haven for your partner's ego. Rather than allying with your partner when he/she is in a feeling frenzy, listen without judgment and invite him/her to rejoin you in the Sanity of Presence.
14. Be guided by your own light—each partner must have a strong connection to Spirit. To avoid becoming trapped in illusions, the following factors are important to consider: do not judge your relationship through anyone else's eyes or values; do not speak ill of your partner; do not keep score; do not compare your partnership with others; do not become a martyr; learn the art of non-attachment; replace jealousy with compassion; do not indulge in "woe-is-us" mentality; and do not push a reluctant partner.

As Maha and David so aptly state: "The key to walking the Esoteric Path of Marriage is learning how to process your own emotions, allowing them to pass through so you no longer identify yourself or your partner as the emotions" (p. 81). I encourage readers to take time pondering this simple but powerful message as found in their sixth chapter, "Slaying the Dragon."

For readers who are interested in exploring the processes of Maha and David in detail, their book outlines exercises that stem from a more spiritual perspective that are worthy of attention. Also, their chapter on communication contains excellent ideas for improving dialogues between couples. For readers interested in specific ways for couples to meditate together, these are presented in the chapter devoted to promoting harmony and unity. In conclusion, Tantric sex is discussed with emphasis on the rise of Kundalini energy, which will be discussed in my next chapter.

Reviewing these, it is clear that three things are basic to healthy relationships: they occur in many ways, including with family members, coworkers, spouses, and friends; the emotional factor, whether with yourself or another, is paramount; and an appropriate balance between masculine and feminine energy within each individual is vital.

How Relationships Developed in My Life

A psychic once told me that when I was born I connected with the natural setting outside the window. This made a great deal of sense because I was born at home in a bed close to a window, and as long as I can remember I always felt more connected to nature and to being outside than I did to family members. In the hot days of summer, I enjoyed sitting in the shade of a large tree in the front yard as well as sitting next to the creek that flowed in a pasture across the street. The loneliness and disconnection I felt from my family was soothed by communing with Mother Nature. Throughout my life, this connection has been important, especially as I grappled with overcoming insufficiencies from childhood.

My early years of loneliness within the family paradoxically paved the way for a positive relationship with the woman my father married, a year and half after my mother died. She was a spinster in her thirties whom we called "Sis" (she had a twin brother and that had been her nickname in her growing-up years). My older sisters didn't take to her, which was understandable, as they had experienced our mother in a different way than I had. My two older brothers related to Sis in a more positive way. As I watched their interactions I knew I wanted to have a good relationship with her. She also had a good relationship with my brother four years younger than I.

Sis had Bohemian ancestry—such descendants are said to be unconventional in appearance and behavior, artistic, and eccentric. In many ways Sis could be described this way. She was an extrovert who interacted with unfamiliar people as if she knew them, with little regard for whether they welcomed her presence or not. Sometimes I was amazed by and enjoyed her behavior with other people, as it was refreshing in contrast to my family's reserved behaviors. Other times, however, I was embarrassed.

She was very creative and a wonderful cook. Prior to her arrival, the bill of fare had been meat, potatoes, and other vegetables, with little seasoning. Sis introduced the family to a wide array of dishes and especially to Italian dishes. She made ravioli from scratch, which later I learned to make. She also was an excellent seamstress, which resulted in ongoing new outfits for me— she and I would go to the city and buy fabrics and patterns for this.

Only on one occasion do I remember Sis losing patience with me and slapping my face. I don't remember what I had done to cause this yet remember I felt devastated and learned a lesson. Of note is that we never discussed the situation, which was the typical family way—emotions were not dealt with and, on rare occasions when they *were* acknowledged, were not handled in a constructive way. This was most problematic, as Sis could have been described as a hysterical person. She would go along in a calm way and, without warning, launch into a diatribe about one thing or another. This was confusing and resulted in temporarily distancing myself from her.

On the brighter side, I felt Sis really cared for me. She was there each day when I came home from school, eager to hear about what had happened that day. She supported and became involved in school activities. When I was in high school I was elected district chairman of the Future Homemakers Association, which involved driving to other towns and sometimes giving a speech. Sis shared that she experienced me as an inspiring teacher and encouraged me to pursue teaching in one way or another. With this encouragement I developed self-confidence about being a leader in my field of expertise. Her caring of and attention to me was refreshing, and I regret not having expressed more appreciation to her.

After being married for about four years, Sis gave birth to a daughter and about eighteen months thereafter a son. Another son was born about four years later. I especially enjoyed having babies and toddlers in the house and watching them learn to walk, talk, and pursue new adventures. Even though she was occupied with her own children, she did not neglect me in any way and continued shopping with me and sewing clothes. I remember in particular the dress she sewed for my senior prom, a lovely blue organza fabric.

When I was in high school I got up early every morning and walked to the Catholic church where I played the organ during mass. The procedure in those days was for parishioners to pay the priest five dollars to say mass for the soul of a deceased person, and I was paid one dollar of the five for playing the organ. When I returned home, Sis always had a hot breakfast ready. She also encouraged me to pursue higher education. When I went to college, I missed being cared for in this way and at first was homesick.

Of course, after I married and did not live close to my family of origin, visits were few and far between. In 1997 my father was terminally ill with a leukemia type of ailment. I flew from New Mexico in the spring to spend a week with him and Sis, knowing that it would probably be the last time. Although he wasn't yet bedridden, he was weak and frail.

One night when I was asleep in an upstairs bedroom, I was wakened by Sis shouting at my dad as they sat in the kitchen. I was startled to say the least and chose to lie quietly while the diatribe continued for some time. When my dad would say anything, it was in a soft and calming tone. The next morning when I went downstairs, he was sitting at the kitchen table. Sis was in the basement doing the laundry. He asked me if I had heard the conversation during the night and I said yes. I then asked him why he remained quiet through most of it and then spoke in a calm tone. He replied that he should have paid more attention through the years to what she was saying and asking of him, and had he been more responsive to her requests, the situation wouldn't be so bad. In other words, when Sis spoke her truth she was not heard, which throughout the years eroded their relationship.

I had never experienced my dad in such a humble, understanding, and emotionally responsible way, which was a huge step for him. For me, it was both a relief and a new and heartfelt appreciation of him. He had lived his life as a chauvinist who believed his way was the right way and should be obeyed. It was as though this was something he needed to admit and make peace with, for himself and hopefully with her, before he died.

A few mornings later, as I was preparing to go to the airport, we both knew it would be the last time we would be together on this earthly plane, and with gratitude and love we gave farewells to each other. When he died the following November, I did not attend the funeral, as I was in graduate school and it was near the end of the semester, with papers due and exams. Yet primarily I did not want to attend because the males in my family tended to drink heavily, and they would be remembering their dad in a way that was much different than mine. I felt Dad knew this from where he was and understood. In fact, shortly after his death, he appeared in a dream and told me my next step was to deal with my mother-in-law, which is exactly what happened. At the beginning of my marriage she thought I was wonderful, but as time went on and my husband and I went through many changes, she targeted me with her frustration.

Since my dad's illness and death, I have only returned to the Midwest one time. One of my sons and one of my daughters accompanied me as I went to confront a male relative regarding sexual abuse. Having prepared for a considerable length of time for this event both by going to therapy and journeying, I was confident and calm. I was ready to speak my truth.

Since I had not told him the purpose of the visit, he asked at the outset if I wanted to borrow money, to which I said no. He and his wife then sat with us in their living room as I told him of his abuse of me that occurred when he was an adolescent. He said he had no recollection of having done so, yet as my son and daughter later pointed out, he did not deny it. Notably his wife said she admired my courage for speaking my truth. However, at the end of the visit, she gave me a card and said I could call her at any time if I needed help with this problem. I felt very disappointed and frustrated by this, as it implied I had the problem and not her husband. I have not seen him since then; however, we exchanged letters a couple of years after the visit in which we expressed caring and understanding of each other, and that meant a great deal to me.

Regarding the rest of the family, we exchange Christmas and sometimes birthday cards. One older sister expressed concern that I had told her grown children about my sexual abuse, which she did not think was the correct thing to do. The other older sister seemed the most concerned that I am a "fallen- away Catholic," yet of late she seems to have softened her stand. Furthermore, I was the first of ten children to get a divorce, which does not fit well into the Catholic way of life. However, more recently, my half-sister divorced her husband—she too had left the Church many years ago. My oldest brother died a year or so after my dad's death, and my other brother and two half-brothers to my knowledge remain devoted to the Catholic Church. No longer having close ties with my family of origin seems right, as it allows me to remain true to myself—a self they have difficulty understanding and relating to.

Sis lived at least a decade after Dad's death. We had a phone conversation when she was on her deathbed, during which she asked me to pray for her. Prior to that time I did not experience her as a religious or spiritual person, yet her request for prayers carried a knowing in her voice that there was life beyond death, and she in her own way was preparing for it. It seemed that a spiritual bond had been actualized in our phone conversation, for which I am grateful. As I remember she died a day or two after our farewell.

Overall, the relationships I had when I was growing up left a great deal to be desired. And as you surmise from what you've read in these pages, I've learned to participate in and create relationships based on sound principles that lead to success and fulfillment. But you may also have noticed an important element missing in this chapter about relationships: sexuality. This subject is so rich that it requires its own chapter—read on.

Knowing and adhering to the truth of who I am took a number of years and many lessons along the way. Doing such involves a unique path for each person. For almost everyone, there are spider times of reflection and ant times of community, during which informative experiences occur. Each of these times is important, and as you travel your path, I wish you many blessings on your endeavors.

WORKS CITED

Brown, M. & Brown, D. (2016). *The esoteric path of marriage: A guide to spiritual enlightenment through relationship.* San Bernardino, CA: Sacred Human Press.

Gottman, J. (1999). *The seven principles for making marriage work.* New York: Harmony Books.

Chapter 9

Sacred Sexuality

SEXUALITY IS INTEGRAL to the return of the feminine, in all of its aspects: physical, emotional, and spiritual. Bringing together what we have explored about balancing feminine and masculine energies, we now look at how this is accomplished sexually.

Many know that sexuality is important to physical health. Christiane Northrup, MD, refers to sexuality as one of the most powerful energies for creating health. In her book, *Women's Bodies, Women's Wisdom* (2006), she states: "We are hardwired from birth for sexual pleasure. It is our birthright" (p. 237). Psychologist Margo Anand extends this concept to spirituality:

> For woman, the road to true sexual liberation consists of walking the sacred path that begins with the first stirring of sexual pleasure in her genitals and ends in a prolonged and thoroughly fulfilling orgasm. With this creative act of cherishing her body, encouraging her own ecstasy, the woman can reconnect with the goddess within, not as some mythical deity, but as the living principle of female wholeness (p. 244).

Anand further states: "The reemergence of the sacred feminine principle goes hand in hand with the rebirth of the feminine pleasure principle, and with the balancing of male and female prerogatives to the experience of sexual pleasure" (p. 244).

When the relationship between female and male roles is balanced—even though each individual displays this in a unique way—the overall result is often referred to as *spiritual*. This is aptly described by authors Richard Rohr and Joseph Martos (1996):

> The spiritually whole person integrates within himself or herself both the masculine and feminine dimensions of the human spirit. She or he is androgynous in the best sense of that term. Neither side dominates because each energizes the other, and each is empowered by the other (p. 16).

In Rohr's book, *Eager to Love*, the specifics of this integration of the feminine and masculine is examined through the life of St. Francis of Assisi and his spiritual companion, St. Clare. It is useful to consider this here, because at first it may be difficult to fully understand the spirituality within sexuality.

In his youth, St. Francis was very much like many others his age. Lustful and materialistic, he desired popularity, alcohol, women, excitement, and power. He demonstrated a typical male approach to life, including interest in the outer world, the rational, the action of things, and an independent stance toward relating to others. However, when his overindulgence didn't result in happiness, he became disillusioned. Eventually he experienced a serious illness during which he almost died. In confronting the reality of death, he questioned his faith and beliefs and ultimately understood that "the only way [to love God] was to hear God's voice in everything: in the song of a bird, in the scream of the mad, in the despair of the leper, and in the embrace of the lovers—that was the way to love God!" (Bartholomew, 1986, p. 155).

With this realization, St. Francis was taking a step toward the feminine energy in his life: exercising his ability to form mental images, pictures, or concepts of what is not actually present in the senses and developing his interest in the soul, deeper feeling states, intuition, harmony, beauty, and relationships with others. Moreover, "to hear God's voice in everything" expands our sense of the paradoxical, because it includes loving even difficult feelings such as terror, sadness, anger, and despair. If the divine is to be seen, heard, and felt in *everything*—including intense sexual experiences—then we must allow such emotions to be what they are and eventually embrace them with love. This is how we pass through the illusion of being "good" and experience and express the trueness of our godlike selves.

It took me a long time to accept and learn this lesson, since for so many decades of my life I sought to be "good," in the sense that I strove to overcome "bad" feelings. Having read about my time of transformation, you probably are not surprised to know it took a great deal of effort on my part to accept the truth of loving my emotions—all of them. Dealing with terror was the biggest challenge. Who in the world, I thought, wants to love the *terror* they feel within themselves? Who wants to love the *rage* they feel inside?

Remember, though, the results from scientific research indicating the role of *neuroplasticity*—the term given the ability of the brain to form new connections at nerve endings where links did not exist or were injured—in transforming dysfunctional patterns. Neuroplasticity actually makes it possible to love one's terror and rage. The OECF (Open Expand Connect and Follow—see Chapter 3) meditation I learned and practiced helped me form new nerve connections in my brain, which eventually resulted in healthy emergence from my years of struggle. Although this is a twenty-first-century concept, those who have meditated throughout millennia have experienced it as well; St. Francis was experiencing it as he meditated on and embraced his emotions.

Paradoxically, both St. Francis and St. Clare contemplated the purposes and meaning in life and both chose celibacy. This was a fruitful and positive choice for others in their time, and it may be the same for some individuals now—"a choice for 'all love' instead of just 'one love.' Such people manifest an eagerness to love that they actually incarnate erotic energy in other ways than physical sexuality" (Rohr: pp. 203-204).

This paradox relates to what was explained in Chapter 3 about Kundalini— the spiritual energy within the body that can be awakened and lead to deep meditation, enlightenment, and bliss, which involves energy physically moving up the central channel of the spine to the psychic center and the top of the head. Such experiences feel like an electric current running up the spine and can occur both during sexual encounters (devoted to spiritual awareness) and when one is alone and in a deep meditative state.

Tantra

Tantra is an ancient Indian tradition of beliefs, meditation, and ritual practices that seek to channel the divine energy of the universe into human consciousness to attain spiritual advancement and self-realization, or *nirvana*. Dating back to Taoism in the fifth century CE, it had a great influence on both Hinduism and Buddhism. These three Eastern traditions are based in the belief of the unity and mutual interrelation of all things and events and the experience of basic oneness. All things are considered interdependent and inseparable parts of this cosmic whole and as, different manifestations of the same ultimate reality.

Similarly, science now shows how our physical bodies are not as dense as they appear—there is more space than density. So it is no surprise that sacred sexuality involves exploring this relationship with inner spaciousness beyond the dense body. When practicing sacred sexuality, we live within the physical world while integrating an experience beyond this world, and the resulting vibration translates into feeling unconditional love for all people and things. From this perspective, sexual ecstasy occurs when our bodies merge with spirit as we dissolve as individuals and become one with everything.

Because Tantra is a spiritual path, it is practiced in a sacred way in which one honors one's partner. A woman's sexual and spiritual energies are called *Shakti*, representing the female energy, which is considered to be limitless, and when awakened this spiritual and sexual energy can be channeled creatively. As Shakti energy rises up to meet her male counterpart—termed *Shiva*—their energies merge to create alchemical bliss.

Tantra from India and Taoism from China both involve balancing masculine and feminine energies. Taoists refer to this as a balancing of yin and yang, with both approaches having a goal of total physical and spiritual union. Tantra makes more use of ceremony, with Taoism being more scientific, with focus on the body and its meridian and energy systems. Tantra, then, is not as much focused on controlling orgasms and constricting muscles; instead there is focus on relaxing into the orgasmic sensations. In contrast, the Taoist approach focuses on control and muscle constriction. Taoist masters have been known to live in vibrant health for over a hundred years due to these sexual practices of ejaculation control.

Although there are similarities between Tantric and Taoist approaches, most practitioners follow only one of the two paths. Ultimately, the key to successfully practicing sacred sexuality is to incorporate both techniques at just the right time. This is valuable because each requires constant awareness, whether through use of Tantric ceremony or Taoist focus on control and muscle constriction. Present-day use of sacred sexuality has the same goal as in the past, but with two primary differences. First, today's practice of sacred sex is a melting pot of the more ancient practices. Second, because of the prevalence of sexual abuse and generations of sexual repression, the present practice of sacred sexuality involves a greater emphasis on sexual issues and healing. This is necessary to ensure a greater quantity and higher quality of energetic ecstasy. Many people worry about sex and feel pressured to have orgasms. What is needed is to relax and heal the inhibitions, fears, and traumas causing the constrictions that prevent the fullest release and best experience possible. In the beginning practice of sacred sexuality, the drive for explosive orgasms must be replaced by the quest for self-discovery and healing.

In *The Art of Sexual Ecstasy: The Path of Sacred Sexuality for Western Lovers* (1989), Anand presents a vast amount of information about Tantric sex. Having studied integral yoga with Swami Satchidananda as well as attending the Arica Institute in New York, founded by South American mystic Oscar Ichazo, she states: "I began to understand the basic principles of how energy functions in the human body, learning how to activate specific energy centers through light, color, chanting sacred sounds, and the visual impact of symbols and images" (p. 5). During this time she discovered Tantra and traveled throughout Asia, Europe, and the U.S., meeting with teachers, shamans, and mystics to learn more about how to integrate sexuality, love, and meditation.

Eventually she began to teach seminars to thousands of people, retaining the Tantric goal of sexual ecstasy while also incorporating new approaches to make this experience more available to people today—with specific emphasis on meditation that is ecstatic and is very similar to the experience of orgasm. She describes these approaches in this way:

> I have seen ecstatic experiences—especially when they are linked with sex—ease or remedy compulsive jealousy, low self-esteem, stress, ailing marriages, timidity, drug dependency, and even bulimia. I also have seen relationships between couples who had become bored—not only with sex but with each other—suddenly blossom into entirely new love affairs, with open, heart-to-heart communication; renewed sexual intimacy; and an underlying spiritual connection that gave their lives together new meaning and fulfillment (p. 8).

In 1978 Anand was a participant in a psychological research project that involved sensory deprivation. For seven days and nights she was cut off from external stimulation, as she wore earplugs with a blindfold placed over her eyes. As she deeply relaxed and focused on thoughts, feelings, and sensations, she experienced a growing peace in which she felt at one with everything. She heard her own voice saying, "Do not look for ecstasy outside yourself. It is already within you" (p. 27).

Anand created an approach for generating ecstatic states that involves a three-step process beginning with the *streaming reflex*, which is the essential part of orgasm. Mobilizing this energy involves welcoming various vibrations and continuing to feel them until they are very pleasurable. In so doing, one learns to experience orgasm as an energy event outside the sexual context and realizes that the true source of pleasure lies within the self and not in a partner. When the streaming reflex is learned, one can then contain the energy and relax into it and expand it and experience the second step of the process—that of *awakening the ecstatic response*, with or without a partner, for long periods of time. The third step is that of *riding the wave of bliss*. The wave of energy released by the streaming reflex is channeled from the genitals up through the body to the head, where orgasmic sensations fill the brain and one learns how to continue this experience from seconds up to an hour or more. Anand states:

> From the Tantric perspective this "orgasm of the brain" greatly stimulates the brain cells and creates a bridge between the right and left hemispheres, fusing the intellect of the left hemisphere with the intuitive faculties of the right. It is this fusion that creates the experience of ecstasy, in which body, mind, heart, and spirit all participate (p. 31).

Again, this involves neuroplasticity, as brain cells create a bridge between the right and left hemispheres. Furthermore, this unleashes the power of the female brain. Barry Komisaruck, a psychology professor at Rutgers University, has done extensive studies (including MRIs) on the brain activity of women during orgasm. In a seven-minute video of the brain of a woman stimulating herself, by the end nearly the entire brain lit up—indicating that most of the brain systems are active at climax. (http://guardianlv.com/2013/05/brainwaves-and-sex/)

Prior to learning the practice of Tantric sex, Anand recommends challenging sexual myths and assumptions—the first of which is the Christian perspective that sex is for creating children. Surely this is an essential and necessary result of sex, yet what is needed is to shift emphasis from procreation to ecstasy. Second, the Western religious tradition of separating the flesh from the spirit results in a condemning and shaming attitude toward sex, which needs to be reformed into honoring and celebrating sex as an act of creation. Also, believing there is a "right" way to make love needs to be replaced. Viewing sex as only a genital affair stands in the way of the wondrous experience of Tantric sex involving a whole body and mind transformation. Furthermore, the myth that intercourse is the only meaningful part of sex needs to be replaced by the experience of full-body orgasms, which include the hands, stomach, shoulders, neck, thighs, belly, and feet that are equally sensitive and capable of orgasmic sensations. The strong belief that one's sexual pleasure depends upon one's partner is another widespread myth. Realizing how the source of one's pleasure is within the self and how each individual is responsible for his/her own pleasure is the first step in learning the art of ecstasy. It is often thought that, for men, orgasm equals ejaculation; however, in developing the ecstatic response, one learns how prolonged pre-ejaculatory pleasure can occur for an extended period of time.

Oddly, some people think Tantra requires celibacy (monks and yogis), with the suppression of orgasm. Yet this is a denial of one of life's most pleasurable activities. Another popular belief is that Tantra is similar to a sexual orgy and promotes hedonistic indulgences.

However, Tantra is the middle path and is neither indulgence nor repression. Tantra teaches us how to explore our sexuality so we can be transformed rather than enslaved by it.

When masculine and feminine energies merge into wholeness, everything is embraced and accepted. Tantra views each human being as an organism, like the environment and the Earth, and infers that all aspects of the self can be integrated, including those that may be rejected and hidden as well as the natural and childlike spirit that loves to play and be ecstatic. The early mystics had their first glimpses of spiritual enlightenment at the moment of orgasm. The unfolding of a Tantric attitude requires being able to love oneself; not feeling guilty about sex; enjoying spontaneity; cultivating pleasure; meditating; not being goal oriented; and allowing surrender.

As authors Morton and Barbara Kelsey state in their excellent book, *The Sacrament of Sexuality: The Spirituality and Psychology of Sex* (1986), "When this kind of loving is present along with and as part of mutual sexual desire within a primary committed relationship, sexual experience can rise to the level of profound religious experience" (p. 126).

Anand presents a step-by-step course detailing various facets of Tantric sex, including:

- how to prolong pleasure by remaining fully aroused while fully relaxed;
- expanding orgasm from a localized sensation to a full-body experience;
- achieving multiple orgasms for both men and women;
- healing a lack of sexual sensation;
- using self-pleasuring alone and with a partner to overcome sexual inhibition and increase sexual self-reliance;
- learning the maps of male and female sexual anatomy;
- recovering from sexual trauma;
- becoming comfortable with safe sex; and

- transforming sexuality into a profound and ecstatic sexual experience.

At the outset of learning about "High Sex," as Anand terms it, students discover the lover within—capable of experiencing the fullness of sexual pleasure rather than looking for the right partner. This begins by students becoming aware of the way they breathe and how deep breathing connects to the sexual centers. As the student settles into the rhythm of deep breathing, he/she invites a memory, image, or feeling to arise of a time when he/she felt totally loved, supported, and protected and then allow the feelings of that time well up inside the heart. Subsequent steps in learning High Sex include:

- opening to trust, in which partners learn to share deep feelings with each other;
- mastering skills that enhance intimacy;
- practices for experiencing the body as a vehicle for transforming consciousness;
- exploring and healing parts of the body that have been wounded;
- releasing pent-up energy;
- the art of erotic touching;
- discovering the inner flute—that is, the movement of energy up through the chakras of the body;
- sexual breathing and pelvic rocking;
- self-pleasuring rituals;
- way of harmonizing one's inner man and inner woman;
- awakening the ecstatic response;
- expanding orgasm from orgasm to ecstasy; and
- riding the wave of bliss.

Anand concludes the book in a down-to-earth way:

> You can apply the elements of the Tantric attitude—self-love, spontaneity, pleasure, and relaxation—in your life as a whole. You can expand your newly found sensuality and aliveness to include not only your beloved but also your family, your place of work, and your environment. The enjoyment you experience in your Sacred Space need not be unconnected to how you feel at the office. High Sex offers you a whole new way of life. You can feel sensual while brushing your teeth, eating your breakfast, or walking down the street. You can feel vibrantly alive while driving a car. The Tantra vision, remember, includes everything, not just your sexuality (p. 424).

I first became acquainted with Tantric sex in the early years of my marriage, when I searched the library of Marquette University for ways to "appropriately" prevent pregnancy—meaning ways that were not considered a sin as defined by the Catholic Church. What I found was a short treatise on Tantric sex that described the male not ejaculating during intercourse. Since this was in a text written by a Jesuit priest, I gave myself permission to give it a try. What resulted was an experience of sex my then-husband and I had not known before. Although there was penetration, we lay in a quiet, motionless embrace for a considerable length of time as waves of energy traveled up through our bodies and between us. We may not have thought of this as spiritual ecstasy at the time, but years later when I read Tantric literature, I realized this is exactly what we experienced.

As I described in Chapter 3, the experience of energy in my pelvis—of power, pleasure, passion, creativity, and positivity—are elements of what I feel when I work with clients and they are speaking their truth; my unspoken truth resonates with their spoken words. I experienced this phenomenon early in my professional career while doing therapy. When clients spoke the truth of their situation—the pain, anguish—and did so with the intent of healing, I would feel the energy of that truth in my pelvis, and I would know that this individual was in the process of healing herself. Said another way, this is what Richard Rohr earlier in this chapter referred to when describing St. Francis's experience of sexual energy being applied in a spiritual way.

Sadly, throughout the centuries of patriarchal repression, most women had no idea that such a thing as female orgasm existed. And women's psyches still struggle with the indoctrination to serve the needs and pleasures of the man, particularly in regard to sex.

Overall Anand's writings truly liberate sexuality for both males and females. As stated in her book *The Art of Sexual Magic* (1996):

> [This book] takes the power of sexuality beyond mere lovemaking by showing how to generate and focus intense sexual energy and use it to achieve personal and spiritual growth. . . . Once lovers learn to channel their intense sexual feelings into mutually envisioned goals, together they will bring about meaningful changes in every aspect of their lives (back cover of book).

However, one area of Anand's perspective that I don't agree with is in reference to serial experiences of lovers. Being a strong believer in committed relationships lasting a lifetime, my sense is that Tantric sex will be that much richer and spiritually expanded for both partners. She does, though, provide appropriate information regarding protection against sexually transmitted diseases and advises taking time to get to know someone before having sexual intercourse.

Because females are often drawn to the practice of Tantric sex first, they may serve as teachers to males. Moreover, females are known to be more patient and can help their partners to slow down while they demonstrate necessary steps such as correct breathing and identifying and sharing emotions.

Meditative Practices That Enhance Sex

Qigong

Relevant to Tantric sex is the application of such practices as Qigong, Tai Chi, and yoga—all of which involve the movement of energy in the body. The Chinese practice of Qigong dates back more than 4,000 years. Archeological evidence indicates the first forms of Qigong involved shamanic rituals and ideas that included postures of meditative practice and gymnastic-type exercises. The earliest known movements were animal dances. Wearing bearskins with four golden eyes on the head, ancient Chinese shamans would dance through a village to drive out pestilence and demons. Villagers wearing masks of various animals would follow. Chinese Qigong masters have been known to live to 120 years old and even beyond. Throughout the years, Qigong has had ongoing evolutionary development and been cited with various names.

According to Lee Holden's historical account:

> Around 450 B.C., Lao Tzu, the founder of Taoism, described breathing techniques in his book *Dao De Jing*, recommending the breath be collected and allowed to descend in the body. Interest in breath and life force (*qi*) was heightened during this period and became the roots of Chinese Medicine, along with the concepts of yin and yang and the five elements (http://www.leeholden.com/announcements/historyof-qigong).

Beginning in the sixteenth century, the nature of Chinese society changed drastically, attributed to the influx of Western ideas, technology, and culture. Contradictory world views greatly influenced the evolution of Qigong. By the twentieth century, Mao Zedong (founder of the People's Republic of China) recognized the conflicting aims and stated, "Chinese medicine is a great treasure house! We must make efforts to uncover it and raise its standards!" (http://en.wikipedia.org/wiki/History_of_qigong). This not only legitimatized traditional Chinese medicine, it also stimulated development of a stronger scientific basis. In the 1950s a Chinese doctor used a method of body cultivation to cure himself of various ailments. He then applied this method to patients and published a book that redefined Qigong without religious or philosophic backgrounds, which was acceptable to the Chinese government. This resulted in the formation of Qigong departments in universities and hospitals that practiced traditional Chinese medicine.

An excellent example of the healing capacity of Qigong is that of Guan- Cheng Sun. When he was a sickly six-year-old, his granduncle tied him upside-down from a tree to cure his digestive and breathing troubles. Raising his arms in a series of motions he sent life energy, or qi, into the lad. After several weeks of these sessions, Guan-Cheng's illness vanished. When he was nine years old his granduncle began teaching him these healing practices. In early adulthood he earned a doctorate in molecular genetics in Japan. He then conducted research at the University of Washington and became a scientist at the Bastyr University Research Institute. In 2015 Dr. Sun had an MRI (magnetic resonance imaging) to record his brain function while engaged in meditation techniques. Furthermore, three miles away at another imaging laboratory, one of his students entered an MRI machine and waited for Dr. Sun to transmit energy to her. He then sent "large-intestine qi," "heart qi," and "kidney qi" to her across town, all of which was recorded and measured. It was found that distinct parts of Dr. Sun's brain were activated when he focused on different organs in her body. Further research is being done to identify how different organs in the body are affected by MRI transmissions. However, another study produced findings that Qigong therapy may help type 2 diabetes patients control blood sugar levels as well as produce psychological benefits (http://www.bastyr.edu/news/general-new- home-page/2012/05/high-tech-imaging-peers-qi).

As a regular weekly attendee at Qigong class in the past, I can attest to the benefits of this practice. Not only is my body more flexible, learning how to direct the flow of energy through my body is remarkable. The "standing like a tree" exercise is a good example. As I stand with knees slightly bent and arms outward as if wrapped around a tree, the upward rise of energy from the earth on my in-breath meets with the downward flow of energy from the heavens on my out-breath, creating a profound effect. During or after a session, one may feel dizzy, nauseous, agitated, or emotional. This results from breathing into parts of the body that store pent-up emotions; however, the space created through Qigong allows such feelings to be released. Masters of this pose can hold the position for hours, yet students are instructed to build up to what is maximum for them by starting with just a few minutes—I was able to do so for ten minutes. Not only is this akin to the experiencing of the rise of Kundalini in Tantric sex, it is appropriate groundwork for such.

More recently I enrolled in an online Qigong class, which provides a daily opportunity to practice. Established by Qigong grandmaster, Dr. Ming Pang, an Eastern trained physician, the class synthesizes elite and secretive Qigong lineages into a comprehensive system with the primary focus on health and healing. It is used in the "medicine-less center" (that is, without the use of standard pharmaceuticals or invasive surgeries) in China. With the application of Qigong daily practice as well as spiritual exercises, a 95% success rate was reported with over 185 diseases, including cancer. Master Mingtong Gu studied with Dr. Pang and brought the Wisdom Healing Qigong methods outside of China through online courses.

Qigong can enhance your health and energy, despite past conditions and external environment. It helps move blockages that result in health challenges and increases energy, health, and longevity when practiced regularly. The video provides the opportunity for practice at one's convenience and is available at a reasonable cost. Visit http://.chicenter.com for more information.

Tai Chi

Tai Chi is a Chinese form of stylized, meditative exercise, characterized by methodical, slow, circular stretching movements and positions of bodily balance. Originally it was practiced as a martial art. As it spread worldwide, countless new styles and offshoots evolved. In the last two decades, Tai Chi classes that focus on health are popular in hospitals, clinics, as well as senior centers. The Mayo Clinic promotes Tai Chi as a positive approach to improving one's health (htttp://www.mayoclinic.org/healthy- lifestyle/stressmanagement/in-depth/tai-chi/art-200045184).

Tai Chi benefits may include:

- decreased stress, anxiety, and depression;
- improved mood;
- improved aerobic capacity;
- increased energy and stamina;
- improved flexibility, balance, and agility; and
- improved muscle strength and definition.

Some research evidence indicates that Tai Chi may also:

- enhance quality of sleep;
- enhance the immune system;
- help lower blood pressure;
- improve joint pain;
- improve symptoms of heart failure;
- improve overall well-being; and
- reduce the risk of falls in older adults.

Anna York, a Tai Chi instructor, had atrophied muscles on the left side of her body due to nerve damage from multiple sclerosis. She used protocols based on a study about Tai Chi movement for restoring gait and balance for those with Parkinson's disease, which helped her develop muscle strength she hadn't felt for decades. She incorporated this approach into her teaching of others, including creating a remarkable DVD, *New Creation Tai Chi-Gong for Walking, Balance, and Strength* (http://annayork.ning.com/). This DVD is available through the Internet. Note that the exercises can be done sitting down if a person has difficulty standing.

Yoga

Yoga is a physical, mental, and spiritual practice developed around the fifth and sixth centuries in India and involves a variety of schools, practices, and goals. Yoga gurus from India introduced yoga to the West in the late- nineteenth and early-twentieth centuries. In the Western world it became popular as a system of physical exercise in the 1980s. However, traditional yoga is more than physical; it has a meditative and spiritual core (https://en.wikipedia.org/wiki/Yoga).

Twenty million people in the United States are yoga devotees. Among the many varieties are yin, power, hatha, and prenatal yoga. Numerous scientific studies report encouraging benefits. The University of Texas - MD Anderson Cancer Center found that yoga helped women undergoing radiation therapy reduce fatigue, improve mental outlook, and regulate the basic stress hormone, cortisol (MD Anderson Center News Release 03/03/2014). The National Center for Complementary and Alternative Medicine in Bethesda, Maryland, used MRI scans and detected more gray matter in certain brain areas in people who regularly practiced yoga as compared with control subjects. (Gray matter is responsible for decision making, seeing, hearing, impulse control, and speech). Other research results indicate that yoga, like Tai Chi:

- Improves mood
- Lowers blood pressure
- Eases depression and anxiety
- Reduces pain
- Prevents falls

Of note is that exercises such as Yoga, Tai Chi, and Qigong—in which body postures involve lowering the head closer to the floor—increase eye pressure. Such postures include downward dog, legs up the wall, standing forward bend, and plow. Gym exercises such as lifting heavy weights and doing pushups can also increase pressure. Consequently, it is important that anyone with glaucoma consult with their ophthalmologist regarding doing such exercises. More information about increased eye pressure/glaucoma/yoga can be found online via a Google search.

Again, females are often the ones who choose meditative practices such as yoga, Tai Chi, and Qigong. Over and over again, as I attend these classes, female attendees by far outnumber the male attendees. Consistently in a class of thirty students, there are fewer than five males.

This chapter has returned our focus to the mystery of life. Information presented here surely doesn't completely address or solve the mystery, yet understanding how energy flows through our bodies is central to the unraveling of what is puzzling. Tantric energy existed in human beings from the time of Adam and Eve—recognizing and honing its use is not only vital to our well-being but also to our evolution into higher consciousness. Many suggestions were given and techniques explored that offer opportunities for you, the reader, to choose what best fits your life, given your past history and the goals you have for your future. It is my hope that you will have the good fortune to seek and find individuals who complement you and with whom you can share a path of discovery in obtaining a higher and more enlightened consciousness.

WORKS CITED

Anand, M. (1989). *The art of sexual ecstasy: The path of sacred sexuality for western lovers.* New York: Jeremy P. Tarcher/Putnam. Anand, M. (1996). *The art of sexual magic.* New York: Jeremy P. Tarcher/Putnam.

Holden, L. (2011). *The history of Qigong.* Retrieved from http://www.leeholden.com/announcements/historyof-qigong

Kelsey, M. & Kelsey, B. (1986). *Sacrament of sexuality: The spirituality and psychology of sex.* Rockport, MA: Element.

Komisaruck, B. Retrieved from http://guardianlv.com/2013/05/brain waves-and-sex/

Mayo Clinic information retrieved from htttp://www.mayo clinic.org/healthy-lifestyle/stressmanagement/in-depth/tai-chi/art2000451

Moore, M. M. (1986). *Bartholomew. I come as a brother: A remembrance of illusions.* Taos, New Mexico: High Mesa Press. Northrup, C. (2015). *Goddesses never age: The secret prescription for radiance, vitality, and well-being.* New York City: Hay House. Northrup, C. (2006). *Women's bodies: Women's wisdom: Creating physical and emotional health and healing.* New York: Bantam Dell. Qigong Master Mingtong Gu information retrieved from http://.chicenter.com

Rohr, R. (2014). *Eager to love: The alternative way of Francis of Assisi.* Cincinnati, OH: Franciscan Media.

Rohr, R. & Martos, J. (1996). *The wild man's journey: Reflections on male spirituality.* Cincinnati, OH: St. Anthony Messenger Press.

Sun, Guan-Cheng information retrieved from http://www.bastyr.edu/news/general-new-home-page/2012/05/high-tech -imaging-peers-qi
Yoga information retrieved from https://en.wikipedia.org/wiki/Yoga and http://.nccih.nih.gov/research/results/spotlight/062013

York, A. information retrieved from http://annayork.ning.com/

Chapter 10

The Eternal Goddess

THROUGHOUT THIS BOOK, you have learned about the goddess within each of us—the ideal of embodied feminine energy, which is ageless and eternal. In the words of Christiane Northrup, MD, from *Goddesses Never Age* (2015):

> The soul is ageless, and it's an expression of the divine, feminine creative force of the universe. The sacred feminine has traditionally been associated with darkness, the body, mystery, fertility, receiving, and the primordial soup—the womb in which all life begins and is nurtured. Every woman is an ageless goddess, an expression of the sacred feminine physical form (p. xi).

As a physician, Northrup shares a great deal of knowledge about the physical body. All bodies, whether male or female, are in a constant state of replenishment as new cells die and new ones are born—we do not have the same physical body we had a few years ago. Scientific research increasingly shows how the aging process can be slowed through mindfulness meditation, exercise, and thinking differently. Cellular breakdown associated with aging occurs due to the accumulation of toxins, which damage tissue and organs. Toxic buildup is exacerbated by scarring of connective tissue caused by physical, emotional, and mental stress.

Females and males who empathically take on the cares of others too often take on other individuals' emotional stress. Specific stress hormones of cortisol and adrenaline are intended to be used when there is immediate threat to physical safety. When they are constantly elevated due to emotional and physical stress, they cause chronic degenerative diseases, including cancer. Stress also inflicts damage on our bodies over time. Antioxidants remedy this, as well as avoiding sugary food (especially when stressed) and limiting the intake of alcohol. Furthermore, physical degeneration of the brain, including memory deterioration, can be attributed to stress, whether from eating too much sugar, chronic worry, or lack of sleep.

Contrary to what many people believe, cognitive decline is not a normal part of aging. In fact the Ohio Longitudinal Study of Aging and Retirement reported that people with positive perceptions about aging live approximately seven and a half years longer than people who do not hold positive perceptions. Furthermore, perception on aging had more of an effect on healthy longevity than having low cholesterol or low body mass.

Another study done with people aged 60 to 90 to determine their "swing time"—the time the foot is off the ground when a person is walking— measures balance and can indicate when someone is frail. The two groups in the study were told to walk so their swing time could be measured. Then they played a computer game. The first group's game had subliminal positive messages such as "wise," "astute," and "accomplished." The second group had subliminal negative messages such as "senile," "dependent," and "diseased." After playing the game, the first group's swing time increased while the second group lost swing time and walked as though they were "senile," "dependent," and "diseased." This change seemed to be completely due to unconscious thoughts and the instant effect of such thoughts on bodily functions.

Northrup concludes: "The most important thing you need to know about your health is that the health of your body and its organs does not exist separate from your emotional well-being, your thoughts, your cultural programming, and your spiritual outlook. *Your thoughts and beliefs are the single most important indicator of your state of health*" (pp. 9-10). Therefore Northrup emphasizes how imperative it is to address health concerns as being caused by emotions and/or thoughts. She recommends we ask the following questions (p. 10):

- What is going on in my life, my thoughts, and my beliefs that I can learn from this situation?
- What is the soul lesson for me here?
- How can I grow from this?

The power of pleasure is integral to good health, since our bodies are wired to repair and renew themselves when we are happy. Cells throughout our body produce a molecule call nitric oxide, which relaxes and widens blood vessel walls and allows more blood to flow through them. Nitric oxide is triggered by laughter, orgasm, eating fruits and vegetables high in antioxidants, meditating, and exercising. Pleasure leads to more pleasure, as life renews itself. Unfortunately, due to our cultural and social heritage, many of us grew up feeling undeserving of pleasure.

Because pleasure comes in many guises, it is to one's benefit to observe each day the simple and memorable pleasures that occur: from petting the cat, walking outdoors, savoring a favorite food, receiving a raise at work, attending an award-winning, delightful stage production, and making love in an ecstatic way. Giving yourself permission to increase moments of pleasure every day is an essential ingredient for vibrant health. Closely related to pleasure is laughter, which has multiple proven benefits: it reduces inflammation, lowers blood pressure, provides greater immunity, improves memory and circulation, reduces pain, and improves blood oxygenation.

Ho'oponopono

What to do when one becomes ill? Western medicine is at its best in dealing with a life-threatening illness, replacing hips, and treating acute physical trauma, such as broken limbs. For other conditions we must turn to our healer within, which involves a holistic mind-body-spirit approach. As Northrup showed, examining one's thoughts and beliefs can have weighty impact. One outstanding method (referred to in Chapter 3) originated in ancient Hawaiian teachings. Termed *Ho'oponopono*, this is a process of letting go of toxic energies within you to allow the impact of divine thoughts, words, deeds, and actions.

Psychologist Dr. Hew Len—referred to as "E"—was employed at the Hawaii State Hospital in the ward where the criminally insane were housed. "E" never saw patients or professionally counseled them. Instead he sat in his office and reviewed their files, and while doing so, he worked on himself. To everyone's amazement, patients began to heal! Author Joe Vitale, in his book *Zero Limits* (2007), quoted Dr. Hew Len:

> After a few months, patients who had been shackled were being allowed to walk freely. . . . Others who had been heavily medicated were getting their medication reduced. And those who had been seen as having no chance of ever being released were being freed. Not only that, the staff began to enjoy coming to work. Absenteeism and turnover disappeared. We ended up with more staff than we needed because patients were being released. . . . Today that ward is closed" (pp. 21-22).

When asked what he was doing to cause these patients to heal, he replied that he was simply cleaning that part of himself that he shared with them. He then explained that total responsibility for your life means that everything in your life—because it is your life—is your responsibility. The entire world is your creation. As stated in Zero Limits:

> Yet the truth is this: If you take complete responsibility for your life, then everything you see, hear, taste, touch, or in any way experience *is* your responsibility because *it is in your life*. That means terrorists, the president, the economy—anything you experience and don't like—is up for you to heal. They don't exist, in a manner of speaking, except as projections from inside you (p. 22).

Notice how this is related to dealing with the shadow side (Chapter 4) of oneself, which in changing yourself, you learn to love yourself.

Dr. Hew Len used Ho'oponopono to heal himself from the inside out (also called *Self I-Dentity Ho'oponopono*) and is encapsulated in the prayer, "I'm sorry. I love you." You don't need to actually feel or believe "I love you" for this to work; you just have to say it and eventually you *will* actually feel and believe it. An expanded version of this is, "I love you (pain in my back); I'm sorry. Please forgive me. Thank You." Additionally one can process emotions in this way: "I love you, my terror. I'm sorry. Please forgive me. Thank you."

I have used this prayer for many years now, for both emotional and health issues. For example, in the mid-1990s I was diagnosed with the beginning stages of macular degeneration and was told by the ophthalmologist I would eventually go blind. When I saw another ophthalmologist for a second opinion, he said recent research results showed that certain supplements could slow down and sometimes stop the worsening of the condition. Needless to say, I began taking the supplements. And after reading the *Zero Limits* book, I began to pray, "I love you, my eyes. I'm sorry. Please forgive me. Thank you." At one point when I went for a routine eye exam, the ophthalmologist was pleased to report that one of my eye tests showed actual improvement—something he had not seen before. Of significance is that when I was first diagnosed with the condition, I wondered what I was not seeing in my life or feeling within me—in other words, what emotion was I repressing? The answer was revealed during my second sabbatical (see Chapter 2).

Recently when I developed a polyp in my right nostril, the doctor prescribed a cortisone nasal spray to shrink it and to avoid surgery. Every day I used the spray and prayed: "I love you, this polyp. I'm sorry. Please forgive me. Thank you." Again I wondered what emotion I might not be dealing with—I then realized how as a child, after my mother died, I developed a sinus condition that required several trips each week to a city fifty miles distant for treatment. I received deeper understanding of those early events during a Brain Dynamics session, where I reconnected with my innocence—an innocence I came into this life with that was impacted by sexual and physical abuse—and I learned to believe good things *can* happen to me. It was suggested that once a day I imagine my inner child enjoying treats—like ice cream or a new dress, thus giving myself more permission to enjoy the innocence of my life.

The first imaging I did was giving my inner child a kitten to play with, followed by imagining her enjoying being on a merry-go-round. The next morning I woke very early and heard doves cooing outside my house—doves have special meaning to me, as they represent peace. I then remembered a vague dream of being with one of my granddaughters who, as a child, had been given many treats. Since I do a shamanic journey every morning when I wake, I proceeded to do so and during the journey I went back to sleep and had an astounding dream in which I was in an upstairs room of a building where a female massage therapist was working on me, who in ordinary reality was unfamiliar to me. She also seemed to be psychologically/spiritually astute. In the latter part of the session, an issue came up that was bothersome to me and I figured we would process it and wanted to do so. I had just opened my blouse—symbolic in that I was going to bare myself to the therapist and process what was troubling me. Just then several women entered the room carrying flowers, and it seemed they were going to arrange them and have photos taken. I was outraged by the intrusion and got up off the table and went to the main female and shouted at her, expressing rage about the intrusion on and interruption of the session. However, when I looked at the clock it was past the hour, and I realized the intruders were probably scheduled to come at that time. So I went back to the table and collected myself. I returned to the main female I had vented anger on and told her it was my process—it was not about her, it was my hatred/rage coming out. She seemed to understand. Next I saw a woman coming in another door that was to the outside of the building; she had to walk along a ledge to enter the room. I thought later how she was a part of me who had gone out on a ledge to vent as I did in the session.

When I woke from this dream I realized how much it was about rage I had repressed in my childhood about not being considered special or worthy of treats. I also realized this was a day of a full moon and how emotions are often closer to the surface, especially since I was born on the eve of full moon. To my good fortune, dreams and journeys are perfect venues for expressing pent-up emotions. And with the practice of Ho'oponopono, the polyp is now hardly visible, with surgery completely out of the question. No matter the health or emotional issue, I find saying this prayer relieves and/or reverses the issue.

In summary Joe Vitale describes Ho'oponopono as viewing life experiences from the perspective that nothing is outside of us.

> When most people pray, they act like they have no power or responsibility. But in Ho'oponopono you are totally responsible. The prayer is to ask for forgiveness for whatever is in you that caused the outer circumstance. The prayer is reconnecting to the divine. The rest is trusting the divine to heal

you. As you heal, so does the outer. Everything, without exception, is inside you (p. 174).

Your inner healer knows that emotions are a potent guidance system that must be recognized, addressed, and taken care of. Exalted emotions such as compassion, joy, love, focusing on the positive, and righteous anger are viewed as promoters of good health.

You've probably figured out by now that the common threads that weave throughout this book are:

- females are more in touch with their feeling states;
- emotional repression can result in illness;
- females can teach males how to recognize and express their emotions effectively; and
- many approaches exist to express our emotions in a healthy and healing way.

How this plays out in life varies from person to person. Northrup describes her personal approach that makes use of the following prayer: "With my spirit and the angels' help, I focus Divine Love throughout my system and bring Divine Love into my (area of the body you are concerned about). I ask that this problem now be resolved with Divine Love, according to the Creator's will" (p. 71). She then draws in her breath, holds it for about four seconds, and then exhales in bursts through her nose. Then she gently focuses on the afflicted part and images Divine Love filling it with light and healing. Northrup emphasizes this is a spiritual process and that she believes when we sincerely ask for Divine help it comes, and Divine Love does the rest of the work.

After making such a request, it is important to pay attention to any guidance that is received. For example, feelings of anger or sadness may occur that are in need of being recognized and released. It is important to remember how the inner healer works in an atmosphere of faith and trust. If you feel doubt or anxiety, the following can be used: "Divine Beloved, change me into someone who trusts my divine guidance and knows that I will be shown the next step" (Northrup, p. 72).

Northrup rightly devotes attention to the seat of female creative powers— the pelvic bowl, whose muscles, connective tissue, and organs include the uterus, ovaries, bladder, urethra, female erotic anatomy, pelvic floor muscles, and large intestine. All creative energy arises from this place. Associated with this area is the second chakra—the body's energy center that manages our relationships with money, sex, and power. This is where impregnation occurs, with the ultimate generating of and birthing of new life. In fact it is the cradle where we access energy for everything we create—whether a piece of art, a relationship, or a human being.

When we don't heed the call of our pelvic energy, we may experience physical problems in that area, including weak pelvic floor muscles that may result in stress incontinence. The remedy for this is to drink plenty of water and do Kegel exercises (see the Mayo Clinic website for instructions).

Final Words on Feminine and Masculine Balance

Many things are changing on planet Earth. Every day we are besieged by news of terrorist activities; increase in homicides; verbal attacks on political personages and from them; increased number of individuals addicted to drugs; trafficking of women and children—most of whom are girls; countless numbers of people who live in abject poverty; immigrants and refugees who drown or are murdered during their attempts to move to a better country; controversies regarding countries allowing individuals to immigrate; and tales of youth and children committing suicide or killing others. Subsequently this time of the feminine rising in partnership with the masculine—both within us and between men and women—is of utmost importance.

Jean Shinoda Bolen, MD, speaks to this in her book *Urgent Message from Mother: Gather the Women, Save the World* (2005). She notes how women have changed the world through collective action—first in obtaining the right to vote and second (known as the Women's Movement) in the pursuit of social, personal, and economic equality. Bolen conjectures that the third change will be (or perhaps already is) the peace movement, with the goal of stopping violence in all forms. One such organization is Gather the Women (http://.gatherthewomen.org), which is a global sisterhood that connects women through circles and creates a safe place in which they share their true selves. This helps members find their voices, claim their power, and celebrate their self-worth, leading to personal and planetary transformation—an ideal embracing both spider times and ant times.

Although Bolen champions collective gatherings of women in which needed changes are identified and pursued, it is of benefit for women to realize they can also effect change on their own. No matter a female's age, economic status, or social standing, she can teach, model, and lead others, males and females, regarding the abilities we possess to create peace. Among multiple options, this can occur via writing articles for newspapers; volunteering to lead adolescent female groups that inform them of their true worth and capacity to grow; mentoring adult women; and contributing to havens for females who are abused. In addition, any and all individual intents and actions generated through self-reflection, prayer, and meditation also affect human consciousness on this planet.

As previously mentioned, the Global Prosperity and Peace Initiative provides an easy and natural way for both females and males to participate in such an organization—the first of this kind ever created in history. There is no charge for membership. One can join the organization as a person who believes in and supports peace endeavors—endeavors that emphasize education, learning to listen without judging, advancing in negotiating skills, and understanding this is about oneness with no division based on sex, race, or creed.

One can be actively involved by becoming a Peace Ambassador and volunteering (from home) two hours each week or more if one so chooses. Recently when I joined, I learned I was the first New Mexico Peace Ambassador. Further information about this organization can be found at http://.ProsperityandPeaceInitiative.org.

Pragmatically one might say, "How can one person change the prevalence of violence?" Consider the meaning of the collective unconscious—the portion of the psyche that houses the accumulated experiences of all preceding generations. Just as we are consciously connected to one another by telecommunications networks capable of establishing immediate linkage from one end of the globe to another, on an unconscious level we are connected by universal imprints of behavior, emotional responses, and potentiality. Moreover, each time demonstration of any of these potentialities falters or fails, its energy ferments and the gathering intensity is transmitted across a web of unconsciousness to the rest of humanity, casting an enormous shadow.

The collective shadow—when composed of the united and strengthened rejections of social groups projected outward onto others—divides the world into black and white, "us and them," the valued and the devalued. It is "a separating and controlling energy of violence," in the words of Twylah Nitsch, which results in scapegoating, racism, and dogmatism and makes peace unattainable. Groups indulging in acts of racial supremacy or religious righteousness are more often than not reenacting the violations of their abusers. Entire wars are waged in defense of "sacred beliefs"; that is, in opposition to atrocities perpetrated by those who have placed themselves in positions of moral superiority.

The individual shadow finds patronage in the collective darkness. There it discovers safety in numbers and an opportunity to align with other shadows in projecting buried feelings onto political or institutional figures or philosophies. Terrorists and anarchists, the Hitlers and the Saddam Husseins, all serve as collective repositories for the darkness we cannot recognize in ourselves. At a certain point, when the projections cast upon an individual or organization reach a critical mass, they erupt. Said another way, an angry teenager wielding a gun is empowered by our collective investment in refusing to acknowledge the hatred dwelling in our own unconscious. When we acknowledge shadow emotions, we connect to them; when we honor them as our own, we can "take back" our projections. In fact, the more of this energy we manage to reclaim, the more we reduce the mass of the collective shadow and the pressure that forces others to release destructive energy.

Not only are we individually capable of siphoning off pressure from the collective unconscious by digesting material from the personal shadow, but by activating archetypal material, we may also be able to propel an alchemical spark through the invisible network of collective consciousness, invigorating psychic expansion and growth. As the archetypal energies of sublimation, altruism, suppression, anticipation, humor, and empathy come forward, they reflect a life lived through individual expression rather than collective repression. Spreading across the collective web, these energies catalyze movement toward individuation—the development of one's unique identity. From this perspective, the archetypal ripening of any individual invigorates the healing of the whole of humanity. And it would defuse the powerlessness felt by people who see no means for impeding the escalation of chaos and violence in the world. Admitting to emotions that have been denied and defended against is the work of heroes and heroines, and at once an act of self-empathy and collective compassion.

Countless religions and philosophies address the spiritual interconnectedness of humankind. Christians tell us the mystical body of Christ reflects a communion of human souls. Teilhard de Chardin, a paleontologist and French Jesuit priest, coined the term *noogenesis* to describe the "concentration and collective march forward of human thought (Teilhard de Chardin, 1969). Whether the link to spirit is formalized through religion or actualized through a belief in an animating principle, it is the factor most in need of attention in today's troubled world.

The portrayal of a unified cosmos increasingly comes forth. Native American Elder of the Bear Clan Lodge, Waynonaha Two Worlds (2001) expresses this unified concept of individual and collective activities in the single image of the spider web:

> We live on a delicate web made of the finest silk. This was woven by Grandmother Spider to hold us all together. Each one of us holds a strand of this web. What happens to one of us happens to us all, from one end of this Turtle Island to the other and beyond (Email communication, September 3, 2001).

As mentioned in the first chapter, spiders symbolize mysticism. They maintain balance between the past and future and are associated with the magic of creation and keeping feminine energy alive and strong. And they are the weavers of destiny. Consequently, whether alone or in a gathering, we each can work toward and envision spider energy weaving a future in which enlivened feminine energy is in balance with enlightened masculine energy, thus creating peace on this worldwide planet—the ultimate of the paradoxical return of the feminine!

To the Divine and Eternal Goddess

Help me to know and learn my soul lessons
Help me to actualize my true self
Give me courage to prevail
Inspire me to love my emotions
Remind me you are always with me
Help me to remember I am supported and loved
Motivate me to cherish how my spiritual endeavors help all others

WORKS CITED

Bolen, J. S. (2005). *Urgent message from mother: Gather the women, save the world.* San Francisco, CA: Conari Press.

de Chardin, T. (1969). *Building the earth.* New York: Avon.

Northrup, C. (2015). *Goddesses never age: The secret prescription for radiance, vitality, and well-being.* New York: Hay House.

Vitale J. & Hew Len, I. (2007). *Zero limits: The secret Hawaiian system for wealth, health, peace, and more.* Hoboken, NJ: John Wiley & Sons. Waynonaha Two Worlds (2001). Email communication, September 3, 2001.

Bibliography

Adler, A. (2012). *Pushing Upward.* Carlsbad, CA: Hay House. Amen, D. G. (2013). *Unleash the Power of the Female Brain: Supercharging Yours for Better Health, Energy, Mood, Focus and Sex.* New York: Harmony Books.

Anand, M. (1989). *The Art of Sexual Ecstasy: The Path of Sacred Sexuality for Western Lovers.* New York: Jeremy P. Tarcher/Putnam. Anand, M. (1996). *The Art of Sexual Magic.* New York: Jeremy P. Tarcher/Putnam.

Barnes, C. (2006). *In search of the Lost Feminine.* Golden, CO: Fulcrum Publishing.

Blum, R. H. (1993). *Book of the Runes.* New York: St. Martin's Press. Bolen, J. S. (2005). *Urgent Message from Mother: Gather the Women, Save the World.* San Francisco, CA: Conari Press. Brown M. & Brown, D. (2016). *The Esoteric Path of Marriage: A*

Guide to Spiritual Enlightenment through Relationship. San Bernardino, CA: Sacred Human Press.

de Chardin, T. (1969). *Building the Earth.* New York: Avon. Egoscue, P. (1998). *Pain Free: A Revolutionary Method for Stopping Chronic Pain.* New York: Bantam Books.

Estes, C. P. (1992). *Women Who Run with the Wolves: Myths and Stories of the Wild Woman Archetype.* New York: Ballantine Books.

Estes, C. P. (2013). *Untie the Strong Woman: Blessed Mother's Immaculate Love for the Wild Soul.* Louisville, CO: Sounds True.
Fraser, N. & Navarro, M. (1996). *Evita: The Real Life of Eva Peron.* New York: W. W. Norton and Company.

Gagan, J. M. (1998). *Journeying: Where Shamanism and Psychology Meet.* Santa Fe, NM: Rio Chama Publications.

Gagan, J.M. (2014). *Grow Up Your Ego: Ten Scientifically Validated Stage to Emotional and Spiritual Maturity.* SantaFe, NM: RioChama Publications.

Germer, C. K. (2009). *The Mindful Path to Self-Compassion: Freeing Yourself from Destructive Thoughts and Emotions.* New York: Guilford Press.

Gottman, J. (1999). *The Seven Principles for Making Marriage Work.* New York: Harmony Books.

Hall, L. B. (2004). *Mary, Mother and Warrior: The Virgin in Spain and in the Americas.* Austin, TX: University of Texas Press. Janvane, F. & Bunker, D. (1979). *Numerology and the Divine Triangle.* Chester, PA: Whitford Press.

Jung, C. J. (1967). *Symbols of Transformation* (2d ed.) in *The Collected Works*, vol. 5 Bollingen series, XX, trans. R. F. C. Hull. Princeton, NJ: Princeton University Press.

Jung, C. J. (1973). *Answer to Job.* Princeton, NJ: Princeton University Press.

Kelsey, M. & Kelsey, B. (1986). *Sacrament of Sexuality: The Spirituality and Psychology of Sex.* Rockport, MA: Element.

Kubler-Ross, E. and Kessler, D. (2014). *On Grief and Grieving: Finding the Meaning through the Five Stages of Loss* (commemorative edition). New York: Scribner.

Moore, M. (1968). *Bartholomew: I Come as a Brother: A Remembrance of Illusions.* Taos, New Mexico: High Mesa Press.

Northrup, C. (2006). *Women's Bodies: Women's Wisdom: Creating Physical and Emotional Health and Healing.* New York: Bantam Dell. Northrup, C. (2015). *Goddesses Never Age: The Secret Prescription for Radiance, Vitality, and Well-being.* New York City: Hay House. Rohr, R. & Martos, J. (1996). *The Wild Man's Journey: Reflections on Male Spirituality.* Cincinnati, OH: St. Anthony Messenger Press. Rohr, R. (2014).*Eager to Love: The Alternative Way of Francis of Assisi.* Cincinnati, OH: Franciscan Media.

Sandburg, S. (2014). *Lean In: Women, Work, and the Will to Lead.* New York: Alfred A. Knopf.

Vaillant, G. E. (1993). *The Wisdom of the Ego.* Cambridge, MA: Harvard University Press.

Vitale, J. & Hew Len, I. (2007). *Zero Limits: The Secret Hawaiian System for Wealth, Health, Peace and More.* Hoboken, New Jersey: John Wiley & Son, Inc.

Vitale, J. (2008). *Expect Miracles: The Missing Secret to Astounding Success.* Toronto/Ontario Canada: Burman Books, Inc.

Weil, A. (1995). *Spontaneous Healing.* New York: Knopf. Wilhelm, R. (trans.) (1950). *The I Ching or Book of Changes: The Richard Wilhelm Translation,* Bollingen series XIX, New York: Princeton University Press.

Wolff, M. (2004). *In Sweet Company: Conversations with Extraordinary Women about Living a Spiritual Life.* San Francisco: Jossey-Bass.

Zimmerman, J. & Coyle, V. (2009). *Way of Council Ancient Wisdom.* Colchester, United Kingdom: Bramble Books.

About the Author

Jeannette Gagan is a licensed psychologist, registered nurse, author, and educator. The relationship between spirituality and emotionality has been of great interest to her since childhood, beginning with her Catholic family. Exposure to more liberal points of view during her undergraduate years kindled new spiritual and psychological perspectives that she gradually integrated into her professional work.

As a nurse Jeannette worked both with cancer patients and in the field of public health. She married and raised five children, taking a long hiatus before returning to complete a master's degree in mental health nursing and a doctorate in counseling psychology. During this training she was introduced to Ericksonian hypnosis, the contemporary approach to altered states of consciousness. Fascination with this topic triggered more study of how such trance states occur historically and cross-culturally, and thus began her love affair with the transformative shamanic experience.

Her own shamanic journeys brought an awareness of early childhood traumas. Through solitude and with a willingness to respond to the call of the unknown, Jeannette persisted in connecting with nature and its healing power. She undertook an apprenticeship with Twylah Nitsch, a Seneca elder, and also trained with the Foundation for Shamanic Studies. In 1998 she published *Journeying: Where Shamanism and Psychology Meet*—a powerful read described by Larry Dossey, MD as: "A landmark application of shamanic wisdom to early developmental wounding, where the ills of society begin. Anyone interested in the future of psychology should read this book."

Jeannette viewed what was historically and theoretically put forth in *Journeying* as just the beginning of an exciting area of study and exploration. Her intellectual and intuitive curiosity led to more extensive examination of the relationship between the ego and early life traumas. After studying ego-growth research, she authored *Grow Up Your Ego: Ten Scientifically Validated Stages to Emotional and Spiritual Maturity*. This award-winning book reveals that not only are the behavioral sciences providing sound evidence of the existence of the ego, but brain imaging techniques are also validating that our brains are hardwired to generate positive emotions. Jeannette celebrates that no matter one's age or situation, our egos can and do grow up—and spiritual growth is a natural accompaniment. *Grow Up Your Ego* not only explains this science in clear, comprehensible terms, it also offers practical exercises to help readers nurture their own growth.

Jeannette's third book, *The Paradoxical Return of the Feminine*, is both a memoir and an opus on self-healing through the awareness of feminine energy. Jeannette weaves in the story of her elderly years, during which she underwent an emotional and spiritual crisis that resulted in closing her therapy practice; experiencing profound loneliness; spending countless days examining her plight; undergoing psychological treatment; and eventually emerging graced with the wisdom of the innate power we each possess to heal ourselves. Now she is dedicated to sharing her voyage with others, emphasizing that if, at age eighty, she could heal, so can anyone! Whether through books, website information, media interviews, or blogs, Jeannette will continue to educate and encourage those willing to read, listen, and learn that we all can grow and heal. In fact, the hope of the world depends upon this!

More information about Jeannette's mission to teach and motivate others can be found at
www.riochamapublications.com

Enjoy More From Jeannette

www.RioChamaPublications.*com/blog*

Grow Up Your Ego: Ten Scientifically Validated Stages to Emotional and Spiritual Maturity

"A practical, useful guide to the development of emotional intelligence."
—Michael J. Gelb, author of
How to Think Like Leonardo Da Vinci and *Brain Power*

Journeying: Where Shamanism and Psychology Meet
From the fertile ground of psychology and the historic matrix of shamanism comes this daring and pioneering template for healing.

"A landmark application of (shamanic) wisdom to early developmental wounding, where the ills of society begin. Anyone interested in the future of psychology should read this book."
—Larry Dossey, MD, author of *Healing Words, The Power of Premonitions* and *The One Mind*

www.ingramcontent.com/pod-product-compliance
Lightning Source LLC
Chambersburg PA
CBHW020500030426
42337CB00011B/168